Only God *Can Turn a* Mess *into a* Message

Tessie Yanchak-Fraysur

ISBN 978-1-64258-845-3 (paperback)
ISBN 978-1-64258-846-0 (digital)

Christian Faith Publishing, Inc.
832 Park Avenue
Meadville, PA 16335
www.christianfaithpublishing.com

Printed in the United States of America

With a special thanks, this book is dedicated with love and deep gratitude to my friend Leigh Evans. You were relentless in not giving up on Darren and me. You guided us through the biggest storm in our life. Your boldness to share your unending faith and love for our Lord lead us down the path of reconciliation. You have weathered an overwhelming storm and have kept your eyes on Christ alone. I thank God for you and bringing you into our lives. In loving memory of your daughter, Michael-Mae Evans, who fought a courageous battle with cancer, now home free!

What a blessing Michael-Mae was to so many, bringing others to the Lord and Salvation.

"She will be waiting for us someday at heaven's gates saying, 'Come on and meet the King of kings in all of His glory!' And we will." - James Robinson

A special thanks to my pastor, Randy Theiss and his lovely wife, Nikki, at Lifehouse Bible church, for teaching God's truth and leading me into a deeper personal relationship with God through Jesus Christ, for the many hours of counseling you gave Darren and I, and teaching us what marriage looks like, God's way.

To the many friendships I have developed at Lifehouse Bible Church--true sisters in Christ.

To Regina Henderson, who took me by the hand, when I walked into Lifehouse Bible Church a total mess, and for all of the hours you spent doing bible studies with me, praying for me, and praying with me for my family.

I pray that the blessings you all have given me through the years will be returned a hundredfold back upon you. Our friendships have been a source of great happiness and encouragement to me.

Dear Reader,

For the first thirty-six years of my life, I had no idea what living a mess, a test, or a trial truly meant. I was raised in a very conservative home in Houston, Texas, where I was raised Catholic. I attended Catholic schools for elementary and junior high school. We moved to Cypress as I was entering high school, where I graduated from Cypress Creek High School. I lived a pretty sheltered life. My parents took us to church *every* Sunday. If we were going on a vacation in the summer, I can guarantee you, my mother had a Catholic Church picked out for us to attend on Sunday, no matter how far we traveled.

I drank alcohol in high school, but never saw drugs until I was in my thirties.

For the first thirty-six years of my life, I lived a very good life. I married the love of my life in 1987, we had our first child DJ in 1990, our second child Dustin in 1991, and our third child Lindsey in 1992. Needless to say, having three children in less than three years was quite overwhelming. My parents lived close by, and my mother, who was like a best friend, was there to help me those first few years, for which I am eternally grateful. My life for the most part was pretty smooth sailing.

I was no saint, but I knew God; and growing up going to Catholic schools, I knew if I confessed my sins, I was forgiven. I had a very close relationship with God. I taught religious education from the time I was a senior in high school, 1982–2000.

When my first three children started school, they went to St. Anne's Catholic School in Tomball, Texas. While they attended school there, I developed many close friendships with the other mothers at the school. I also did Bible Study Fellowship (BSF) with a few neighbors where I also developed many more close friendships. You could say that this time in my life, I was surrounded by an abundance of Christian women, many of which I developed very close friendships with. Yes, hindsight, I see it was part of God's plan, because I was going to really need those Christian women in the next few years.

On May 22, 2000, I received the worst phone call you could ever imagine. My husband, Dennis, forty-one years old, passed out at work; and they were calling an ambulance. They were taking him to Tomball Hospital. I met the ambulance at the hospital; they did an EKG and told us that he had suffered a mild heart attack, and they would be doing an angioplasty the next morning. I spent the night at the hospital, while friends had the children. The next morning, I left the hospital around 6:00 a.m. to run to the house to pick up a change of clothes and toiletries for Dennis's hospital stay. On the way back to the hospital, I stopped at HEB. I ran into my children's kindergarten teacher in the parking lot and told her that Dennis had suffered a mild heart attack and to put him on the prayer list at the school/church. By the time I got settled back into the hospital room with Dennis, a nurse came in and said that we had a lot of visitors, too many to come into the room, and that I would have to go to the waiting area to visit with them. While I stood in the waiting area talking to several of my closest friends from the elementary school my children had attended, I heard code blue on the intercom, but didn't give it much thought. The next thing I knew, the nurses were asking me to come into a private office with my parents, sister, and Dennis's family. As they proceeded to talk to me, I'm thinking, *They are going to ask permission to do open heart surgery.* As they were circle talking, I began to understand that they were trying to tell me he had passed away, and they had done all they could. In total shock, I thought, *How could this happen? We are in a hospital, and people shouldn't die from a heart attack while under a doctor's care, in the hospital.*

At thirty-six years old, in total shock and totally devastated, I left the hospital, a widow, to go home and tell my three small children that their daddy had died and gone to heaven.

Not even a month later, my grandmother passed away from leukemia, on Father's Day. Then, two months later, my mother was diagnosed with lung cancer and told she probably only had six months to live. She lived a few short years doing a study program at MD Anderson.

By this time, I had met a wonderful man, Darren Fraysur. He was the most compassionate person I had ever met. He had a heart of gold and was always doing something for someone. He had come over to help fix some plumbing issues at my home and won the hearts of my children. I think I won his heart with my cooking. Seriously, he was still a bachelor at thirty-nine years old, so he would eat anything. The boys were asking him to come to their peewee football games, and he helped put up Christmas lights our first Christmas without Dennis. He became what I thought of as a mentor to the children. But through the course of that first year, we fell in love. We got married in 2003 and had our daughter Leah in 2004.

Needless to say, he married a woman that was totally grief-stricken and an emotional mess. We moved to Hempstead, Texas, in 2005, to start our new chapter in life. I started drinking to numb the pain of the loss of my husband and mother. Darren at this time was not a drinker. He had told me when I first met him that he was an alcoholic, but he wasn't attending meetings.

As the years passed, Darren started having a beer or two. My drinking went from just drinking beer to hard liquor. Needless to say, our drinking increased through the next several years. Well as you can imagine, our lives started spinning out of control.

As our older children were entering high school, I started letting them drink an occasional beer or two. There was actually a group of moms that we thought it would be okay for them to drink while under adult supervision, thinking we were doing the kids a favor by monitoring their drinking and taking their keys away and keeping them safe. Well, that worked for some of the kids, but not for my boys. The drinking led to more drinking that then lead to drugs and making poor choices.

As Darren's drinking increased, which led him to a relapse of alcoholism, taking drugs and crystal meth for him.

In 2013, I slipped and fell. I cracked my hip, twisted my ankle, and hurt my back and neck. Twenty-eight days after my fall, I went paralyzed from the neck down, due to spinal stenosis, and the spinal fluid had leaked out of the vertebra in my neck that caused the paralysis. I had surgery with a metal plate put in my neck with eight screws. I was prescribed way too much medicine and was overmedicated. During my recovery, Darren's meth use turned into a full-blown meth addiction. We had one of his family members living with us that was also using meth, and I would later find out he was also a drug dealer. Our nine-year-old daughter Leah found the meth, which is how I found out about the meth use. Our lives at this point had become an unmanageable mess. Darren's personality totally changed and he became verbally abusive. I could no longer live this life any longer, and I filed for divorce.

This is the story of my family's struggle to overcome addiction and all the emotional damage from 2000 to 2014. You can only imagine the miraculous restoration we needed to experience. No matter how much pain, disappointment, or situation has placed you in that deep dark place in your life, there is a way to come into the light of healing and restoration. By applying God's Word, we turned our mess, our tests, and our trials into a beautiful message, testimonies, triumph, and victory.

It has never been my intention to blame anyone for what happened in my past. It is too easy to point out someone else's faults, but we have to remember we all have them. No one is perfect; it's cruel and unfair to hold anyone forever accountable for the mistakes they have made. We have to forgive and let those things go and take responsibility for our lives now. We have to move on. It's my goal to show how applying the Word of God can turn a mess into a message, a test into a testimony, a trial into a triumph, and a victim into a victory. I want to point you toward the source of all restoration and wholeness, God's Word, the Bible.

This is a true story; some of the names have been changed or left out to protect the privacy of people.

This book will show the turning point in my life that started my climb out of darkness. I am starting at the point of the deepest darkness I was living in, in order to fully explain what drove me to the point of recognizing I could no longer live like this and getting help. The help I found was applying God's Word to my life, listening to the Holy Spirit, and moving my feet when I was led too. The facts are what they are, and I cannot leave them out because they are crucial to the story. I feel the entire story should be told in order to prove that once you recognize the darkness for what it is, it is possible to walk out of it and to the light for the rest of your life.

This book is about my life, but it is not so much about me as it is about living in darkness and in the invisible war and spiritual warfare and finding true light and spiritual victory. We have all been there and are all in the battle against the enemy, Satan. Because of the overwhelming number of people who experienced similar or far worse emotional hurt than I did and because so many have given up the battle, because they don't know how to engage the enemy and win, I'm telling my story so that they too can find a way out of the darkness of their lives or their past and onto the path of healing and wholeness that awaits them. I desperately needed restoration, and I found it. And not only that but I also found transformation I never dreamed possible. If I can find it and if Darren and I were able to restore our marriage, anyone who wants can find it, too, with God and his Word.

This book is for anyone who is struggling in any area of their life. You will learn what I have learned—that calling on Jesus is the only way to get through when you are in the middle of a big ol' mess. The Bible has a clear plan and instructions and you too can make it through. Reading God's Word, the Bible, and following *His* plan is an amazing journey to freedom.

I'm a little nervous about releasing this book. It's not easy to put everything out there like I have done here, sharing my family's deepest, darkest secrets.

Join me in putting your feet on the solid ground of our Savior, Jesus, and take the first step to hope, healing, and strength in the middle of the mess. With Jesus, you too can turn your mess into a message. I have prayed that this book will bring freedom, healing, comfort, peace, restoration, transformation, and sense of high purpose God has for each one who reads it. To all who desire to receive all that, may God bless and be with you.

Sincerely,
Tessie

Chapter 1

Why Me, God?

I NEVER DREAMED I WOULD encounter the darkness that I went through after I was well into my thirties. And I certainly never imagined I would be writing a book about it. I have journaled for years as a way of getting things off my chest. Writing out what was going on in my life was a way of getting rid of the baggage, I guess. It also gave me some quiet time alone with God. In some ways, I believe in my early years that it was my way of praying.

Journaling was a way of breathing life back into me. In fact, I felt suffocated if I didn't have time to journal every day. Journaling always brought freedom to my heart and soul and peace to my tormented mind—even if only temporarily. I would write about the things happening in my life and the negative emotions I struggled to overcome. Writing released me and kept me alive. I often have a hard time speaking my thoughts or praying out loud. There were many times that I would hear from the Holy Spirit as I was writing and would be given direction for my next step or answers to issues I was facing.

I tried as hard as I could to overcome situations I was given to deal with and to overcome them. I often wondered, *Why me, God? Why can't I be like other people who never had to struggle as I have?* I clearly remember the day in my midthirties that became a turning point in my life. It started with the terrible tragedy of losing my husband of fifteen years, to a sudden heart attack, leaving me a widow with three small children. At this point, I tried the "fake it till you make it" approach. I found that my three small children would feed off my emotions. If I was upset and crying, they would be upset and crying. If I was happy, they seemed to be happy.

I did a grief recovery class and did as the book told me to. If I was told it was time to clean out the closet, that's what I did. I would read the Bible about grief and I read the passage in Ecclesiastes about there being a time to weep, a time to laugh, a time to mourn, and a time to dance. I would try to apply that to my life. I felt like God was telling me, "Enough with the mourning. Do you have faith? It's time to move on."

This peace was short-lived. In the next few years, I found myself in the deepest darkest pit of depression and stayed there for several years. The trying to "fake it till you make it" was just not working after the death of my mother.

Chapter 2

Daughters of the Almighty King: What a Special Sisterhood Indeed!

*She is more precious than jewels, and nothing
you desire can compare with her.*
—Proverbs 3:15

A friend loves at all times and a brother is born for adversity.
—Proverbs 17:17

THE ONE SAVING GRACE I had was wonderful friendships. I have been blessed with the most amazing friends through the years. Without wonderful girlfriends, there is no way I would have made it this far.

The word "sisterhood" can bring up fond memories for many. To some, it means being a part of a sorority, while to others, it means being a biological sister. In both instances, there is a sense of closeness and loyalty. The Bible paints a beautiful picture of sisterhood. It gives us beautiful illustrations such as Mary (mother of Jesus) visiting Elizabeth and leaving encouraged in what God has called her to do. It shows the young woman in the Song of Solomon being celebrated by her peers who offer caution when needed but also joy and excitement in her newfound love. It tells of Esther's maids fasting with her on behalf of the Jewish people.

There is something to be said about women helping women. Only another woman can truly understand some of the trials we as women endure. God has brought some really wonderful women into my life through the years, during the trials in my life, when I needed them the most.

This is sisterhood in Christ. In my own experience, I've found that sisters in Christ, princesses of the almighty King, is a group of women encouraging, supporting, praying, fasting, laughing, comforting, counseling, correcting, and lifting up one another. I recall memories of sharing God-given dreams and encouraging one another to move beyond our fears to obtain it. My sisters have held me accountable to give God my absolute best and have loved me despite my flaws, they let me know when I need to straighten my crown, and we laugh about it. When the world sees this type of sisterhood, it marvels at it and desires to have the same thing. Strive to live a life of true sisterhood before the world and be prepared to watch God draw other women in to share the same experiences.

Some of these sisters in Christ I was given by birth (I have the best sisters and sisters-in-laws known to man), some I have been friends with for over thirty-five years (who I met when I was in high school), others I met through my children (the mothers of my children's friends in school), and some I met in church and in Bible study. I truly believe God brings the right sisters to you at the right time. What a beautiful gift—the gift of sisterhood.

With these sisters in Christ, I have witnessed competitiveness and selfishness give way to survival through unity, kinship, and an inevitable bond of trust and loyalty. We can be a united front among others, and we know that in a pinch or, worse yet, in an emergency, we can depend upon one another for our rescue in the face discouragement and despair.

Sisters encourage each other at all times.

My desire to be the sister in Christ that God wants me to be had me open up my Bible and dig around to see what the Lord says to us about encouraging each other. As I read passage after passage, I was struck by how vital this expression of love is for God's people. In one sense, encouragement is like oxygen in the life of our fellow sisters. It helps mend broken hearts and clear minds and hands inspired to serve.

Why Do Women Need Encouragement?

God commanded that his people encourage each other because he knows we need it. In the Gospel of John, Jesus warned that "in this world you will have trouble," which he then followed with a much-needed encouragement: "But take heart; I have overcome the world" (John 16:33).

We live in a broken world where everything calls us toward selfishness and despair. Sin steals joy, our bodies break down, our plans falter, our dreams die, our resolves weaken, and our perspective dims. We are promised suffering (1 Peter 4:12), persecution (John 15:20; 2 Timothy 3:12), and trials of various kinds (James 1:2–3).

When encouragement from others is absent from the life of God's people, they will feel unloved, unimportant, useless, and forgotten. God knows his people are in need of grace-filled reminders, so he calls us to encourage each other every day until his Son returns (Hebrew 3:13).

What Is Encouragement?

Biblical encouragement isn't focused on complementing someone's outfit or telling them how good their homemade salsa tastes. That kind of encouragement is important, but the encouragement the scriptures refer to explicitly is Christian encouragement.

Encouragement is shared with the hopes that it will lift someone's heart toward the Lord (Colossians 4:8). It points out evidences of grace in another's life to help them see that God is using them. It points a person to God's promises that assure them that all they face is under his control.

The New Testament reveals that encouragement was a regular part of the early church's life together (Acts 13:15, 16:40, 18:27, 20:1–2, 27:36). They shared scripture-saturated words with each other to spur one another on in faith (Acts 14:22), hope (Romans 15:4), unity (Romans 15:5; Colossian 2:2), joy (Acts 15:31), strength (Acts 15:32), fruitfulness (Hebrew 10:24–25), faithfulness

(1 Thessalonian 2:12), perseverance (Hebrew 10:25), and the certainty of Christ's return (1 Thessalonian 4:18).

Encouragement was and is an essential way of extending grace to each other.

How Do I Grow in Being an Encouragement to Others?

There isn't only one "right way" to encourage each other, but here are a few ideas to help you get started.

Pray for God to make you an encourager. Ask him to give you a heart that loves others and creativity to know how to show it. Ask him to help you die to self-centeredness and grow in a desire to build others up. Because God delights in helping his people obey his commands, we can trust that his Spirit will teach us how to bless others for his glory and their spiritual good.

Ask God to make you like him. Barnabas was nicknamed the "son of encouragement" by the early church (Acts 4:36). He was the kind of guy you wanted to have around as you were serving the Lord. He wasn't just a spiritual cheerleader, but he was a man of great conviction who wanted to see the church flourish and did all he could to make it happen. Ask God to give you a heart like Barnabas.

Make encouragement a daily discipline. For some of us, encouragement comes naturally, whereas for others, not so much. I have a reminder in my calendar each day to send someone an encouraging note, e-mail, text, or phone call. I need this reminder to pause, pray, and then intentionally try to spur someone on in Christ.

Pray for God to show you who to encourage. Ask God to bring someone to mind that you should reach out to. Make a list of scriptures that God has used to bless you personally or an excerpt from something you read in your daily devotional. Read the Psalms, Romans 8, and the gospels. Find and share riches of God's grace with others.

Be specific in what you say. I received a note recently from a friend that included two very specific ways she had seen evidences of grace in my life. When I read them, I was humbled and reminded of the fact that God does actually work in and through me. I needed that.

Pray that God would create encouragement in you. Ask God to make you one that loves others in specific, tangible ways like encouragement. Ask God to use you to help fan that flame. Don't get discouraged if people don't return your encouragement (Matthew 6:3–4; Ephesians 6:3–8) or if you don't see fruit from it (Galatians 6:9–10). Creating a culture that glorifies God takes a long time, lots of prayers, and abundant grace. I encourage you to keep at it.

Get started. What sister can you encourage right now? Who has blessed you recently that you can thank? What verse can you share with them? How might God use it?

Sisters love each other as like-minded women who deeply understand each other's joys and challenges in our unique lifestyles, like no one else.

Such is the nature of teamwork, where the combined efforts of many produce much. Women helping women, as the generations were instructed in Titus 2, produces godly wisdom and achievement. It helps us to begin strong, accelerate fast, and finish well. Where combined seeds of investment are planted, a multiple return is reaped.

I encourage you to pray for the sisters Christ has for you, that your paths will cross, and that you can be a light to each other in the times of need.

Chapter 3

Lovingly Taken Care of by God

A father to the fatherless, a defender of widows,
is God in his holy dwelling.

—Psalm 68:5

WHEN I THINK OF "LOVINGLY being taken care of by God," the first thing I think of is the year 2000. I was thirty-six years old and widowed with three small children. God showed me he cares for all, but he seems to have a soft spot for widows and the fatherless.

After losing my husband of fifteen years and the father of my three small children, God used so many people to be his hands and feet to carry us through that most difficult time in our life.

My three children slept with me those first few months after Dennis's death. Every night, I would read scripture in the Bible to them and to myself of God's promise to take care of the widow and fatherless.

Throughout the entire Bible, God has placed a high value on the importance of caring for widows among the people of God. In fact, the Bible says that God himself takes special interest in the plight of widow and her children. There are seventy-six verses in the Bible about the widow and the fatherless.

The following are just a few of my favorites:

> Father of the fatherless and protector of widows is God in his holy dwelling. (Psalm 68:5)
> God commands us to protect and care for orphans and widows. (Psalm 82:3)
> Therefore I tell you, do not worry about your life, what you will eat or drink; or about your body, what you will wear. Is not life more than food, and the body more than clothes? Look at the birds of the air; they do not sow or reap or store away in barns, and yet your heavenly Father feeds them. Are you not much more valuable than they? Can any one of you by worrying add a single hour to your life? (Matthew 6:25–27)
> The Lord tears down the house of the proud but maintains the widow's boundaries. (Proverbs 15:25)

But the means God uses to protect and maintain widows is often his own people. That's why we're given the following instructions throughout the Bible:

> Learn to do good; seek justice, correct oppression; bring justice to the fatherless, plead the widow's cause. (Isaiah 1:17)
> Thus says the Lord: Do justice and righteousness, and deliver from the hand of the oppressor him who has been robbed. And do no wrong or violence to the resident alien, the fatherless, and the widow. (Jeremiah 22:3)
> He executes justice for the orphan and the widow and shows His love for the alien by giving him food and clothing. (Deuteronomy 10:18)
> You shall not afflict any widow or orphan. (Exodus 22:22)

It's not surprising that the first ministry to arise in the church in Jerusalem was a ministry led by the first seven deacons to oversee the distribution of food to widows who some felt were in need. The church still has a responsibility today to care for widows. James puts it this way,

> Religion that is pure and undefiled before God, the Father, is this: to visit orphans and widows in their affliction, and to keep oneself unstained from the world. (James 1:27)

Reading these scriptures gave me such comfort and gave us hope. I wasn't sure how he was going to take care of us, but I knew he would, and he *did*.

God used everyone we knew to be his hands and feet to carry us through, emotionally, spiritually, and financially. We had so many friends who supported us through that first year. We had dinner cooked by friends and brought to us every night for two months. I would go to the grocery store, and there always seem to be someone in the store who knew us that would offer to pay for our groceries. A friend of ours had a landscaping business and sent his crew over once a week to mow my yard for a year. Friends were sending us gift cards and clothes that they would go buy for my children. We were adopted at Christmas by several families so that my children would have gifts to open on Christmas Day. The outpour of love was overwhelming. When I look back at that awful time in my life, I have to say it was one of the most beautiful times in my life, seeing God work through so many people doing exactly what the scripture called them to do.

I had such a special bond with so many friends who I like to refer to today as my sisters in Christ. They did as I described in the previous chapter, daughters of the almighty King—a special sisterhood indeed. They encouraged me at all times. They were with me each step of the way for that first year. They made sure that I had plans with them on those Friday nights for that first year, which was the hardest for me.

When my husband passed, we didn't have life insurance. We had a family friend put together a benefit that raised more than double his life insurance policy that we had cashed in after our third child was born to pay off bills so I would not have to work full time.

It is so obvious to me that the people in my life at that time were Christians who knew God's Word and command to take care and provide for the widow and fatherless.

You may not be widowed or fatherless, but I am here to tell you that God is lovingly wanting to take care of all his children. No matter what you're going through today, rest assured that God is faithful in his Word and will lovingly take care of you and me! You just need to call on him. He is waiting for you with his arms wide open.

Today, when I need confirmation of faith, it helps to think back on this time in my life when God was faithful to his Word. When I look back at this time in my life, I realized it was not only one of the hardest but also one of the most beautiful times in my life.

The Bible defines faith as "being sure of what we hope for and certain of what we do not see" (Hebrews 11:1). Thus, biblical faith is a channel of living trust—an assurance—that stretches from man to God. In other words, it is the object of faith that renders faith faithful.

Furthermore, faith is the assurance that God's promises will never fail. Hebrews 11 underscores the fact that we trust God to fulfill his promises for the future (the unseen) based on what he has already fulfilled in the past. Thus, our faith is not blind, but based on God's proven faithfulness. Looking back on my life, I can see God's unending faithfulness in everything I have encountered.

Chapter 4

Cancer Sucks

CANCER IS THE ONE WORD no one wants to hear. I have a T-shirt in my closet that says "Cancer Sucks." Cancer is everywhere.

I will never forget the day my mom was diagnosed with lung cancer, and we were told she would probably only have six months to live. The doctors told us that "she will die" from this. I broke down and literally lost it. I ran out of the room at MD Anderson screaming and crying, running as fast as I could down the hallway after the doctors gave us this horrifying—heartbreaking—news. I thought, *No, God. You just took my husband a few months ago. You cannot take my mother too.*

My mother was also one of my best friends. We shared everything together. Even as a teenager in high school, my mother and I had a very unique relationship. I could go to her with any problem I had, and she always had a listening ear and some of the best advice I ever received.

Then, when I started dating, she always let me make my own decisions on who I dated. Luckily, she always seemed to like my choices in boyfriends. She really loved the choice of the man I chose to marry. She and my first husband, Dennis, had a very special relationship. I don't think she could have loved him any more if he was her own son, and he loved her back in the same way.

Before Dennis's death, we got together every Sunday after church for a family dinner. Dennis would usually be throwing some-

24

thing on the pit or my dad would barbeque a brisket. One thing was certain, we would be eating somewhere on Sunday afternoon.

My mother helped me when I needed her the most, after having three babies in 2.5 years, she was there to help me in raising these babies. I don't know what I would have done those first five years without her help. My children adored their MawMaw, and she adored them. They were her first and only grandchildren before she passed away. Now that I am a MawMaw, I completely understand that love that you only have for your grandchildren. It's a love that is unexplainable, pure, and true. I've read recently that being a grandparent is the best because you aren't responsible for their mistakes—that's their parents' responsibility. So I guess that's why being a grandparent is so special, no responsibilities, just good time fun.

Then after Dennis passed away, my mother was with us day and night for the first few months. Looking back, I don't think she grieved his death right away. She was too busy worrying about me and my kids, worrying about how we were going to make it emotionally and financially.

Sometimes I wonder if the stress she lived with in her life time caused her cancer and early death at only a little over sixty years old. I know the stress of Dennis's death took a toll on her, especially after I met Darren and started riding on the back of a motorcycle. She just didn't understand how I could get on the back of that motorcycle and risk losing my life and leaving my children without any parent at all. Hindsight, I see her genuine concern, as I am a grandmother now as well.

After my mother was diagnosed with cancer, I prayed like I had never before. I prayed for her healing. I prayed for a miracle. We took her to several healing masses, desperate for any type of cure we could find. She did chemo and radiation. Both of which in themselves almost killed her. Then when the pet scan showed, it had metastasized to other parts of her body. The only choice she had was a study program. None of these protocols saved her life.

The lyrics to the song *The Scientist* by Coldplay caught my attention during that time. The lyrics that caught me most were, "I was just guessing, at numbers and figures, pulling the puzzle apart.

Questions of science, science and progress, do not speak as loud as my heart." We were talking to all of these doctors and specialists; asking questions and looking at statistics, new trials, new organic diets, and anything to save her. But science did *not* speak as loud as my heart. Nothing can express the pain that goes with loosing someone you love.

Watching my mother die of cancer was one of the hardest things I have ever been through. I wanted so badly to take her pain and suffering away. I wanted to take any sadness, fear, or anxiety she had. I just wanted so desperately for her to be healed.

My sisters, brother, and I were all in bed with our mother when she took that last breath. Those last few days were absolute torture for us to all watch, as she struggled to breathe. It looked like she was literally suffocating, something I pray I never have to witness again in my lifetime.

After God took my mother, after all the unanswered prayers for her healing, I got so angry with God. I quit going to church. I quit going to Bible studies, and I turned my back on God. I thought God was such a mean and untrusting God. I was so angry at God for taking my mother away from me. God obviously didn't love me or he would not have taken my mother and my husband from me. All I could think about was all the good she had done in her life and wonder why God would take someone so good, who had so much to offer, and leave so many bad people here on earth who just go around hurting others. I still needed my mom, even more now that I was a widow. My children needed their MawMaw. I felt deep down that God could have taken someone else's mother. After all, he had just taken my husband a few short years earlier, not to mention that I had several friends who had both their husbands and mothers, and now I had neither. It just didn't seem fair and certainly didn't make any sense to me at all.

This is where my life started becoming a total mess. I started drinking to help numb the pain. I started suffering from depression for the first time in my life. Until this point in my life, I didn't understand depression at all. I was totally against anyone I knew who were taking antidepressants. My thoughts were, *Come on, folks. Get a grip on life. Pull you boots up and keep on walking. Nothing in life could be that bad. Well, never say never.* At this point, I was put on antidepressants.

Today, over ten years later, I can honestly tell you that science did not save my mother; however, God did. It took me years to realize that. I know my mom is in heaven with God. My prayers that I thought were unanswered were answered in the best way possible. Her miraculous healing happened as soon as she crossed over to the pearly gates of heaven. She is no longer suffering any physical illness, and I know she is watching over me and my family. I also know that she is doing good things in the kingdom of heaven, and that's what God needed her for. I don't think our work is done when we leave this earth. I feel God has a purpose for us in heaven as well. I'm not sure what it is, but I know it must be very important, because the people that have been taken out of my life and gone to heaven are truly very special people.

Chapter 5

Enough Love in My Heart
to Love Again

So I would have young widows marry, bear children, manage households, and give the adversary no occasion for slander.
—1 Timothy 5:14

By the time my mother passed away, I had met Darren. I met him after my husband's death, at the benefit that was given for the kids and me. After the benefit, he would call, occasionally checking on me and the kids. I could tell in talking to him he was a man with a huge heart and truly cared about others.

One night while I was cooking dinner, the kids were in getting their baths and not sure what they did, but they were screaming for me to come. There was a problem. Boy, was there a problem. We had water shooting out of the wall where the faucet which was now in the tub. With no way of turning off the water, I was in a panic.

My grandmother had passed away the day before, and my parents were at her house taking care of some business. I was in panic mode not knowing what to do. About that time the phone rang, it was Darren calling to check on us. He could tell by the panic in my voice something was wrong. I told him, "Yes, I need help. My dad is across town at my grandmother's, and I have no idea how to fix this problem."

Darren came to rescue and fixed our plumbing issue. Being that I had just made dinner, I invited him to stay and eat. I told him that at least I could feed him for his troubles. He stayed and had dinner with us, and I found myself laughing for the first time in a very long time. He had the kids laughing, and we were all enjoying ourselves, which was a pleasant change for us.

Before Darren left that night, the boys asked him if he would like to come to their peewee football game the next night. The boys being a year apart played on the same little league football team, and Lindsey was one of their cheerleaders. We could hear him coming down the road, from miles away, as he approached the football stadium, as his Harley Davidson motorcycle had some really *loud* pipes. The sound of those loud pipes on that motorcycle soon became one of my favorite sounds.

Darren started spending a lot of time with the kids and me. He helped us that first Christmas after Dennis's death put up our Christmas tree and lights on the house. He noticed that Dennis had a Lionel Train set in our game room, and he also had some pieces of an old Lionel Train at his house. He and the boys spent the next few nights putting the pieces of both of the collection of train together under our Christmas tree. He had become quite the mentor to my kids.

As the months went on, we fell in love.

My life with Darren has been definitely exciting. He lives in the moment and by the seat of his pants. This was definitely different for me, as I had lived a very conservative life with my first husband.

Darren having a Harley David motorcycle was something I had never experienced. I had never rode or drove a motorcycle before. Once I got on the back of that motorcycle, and he took me down roads I had never been down, I found an escape that I truly loved—a place where I was no longer known as a widow. I started dressing the part as well, all leathered up and exploring new adventures. My family and friends were not too sure of what to think of my new lifestyle. I was told by several family members and close friends that I looked like June Cleaver, all dressed up in leather and posing as a "motorcycle chick." Some told me that they saw me as June Cleaver turning into Sharon Osborn. I just knew we were having the time of our lives.

Darren was not a drinker at this time. I loved a cold beer and was drinking more of them to numb my pain of grief. I think I was drinking more at this time of my life than I did in college.

As time went on and we were getting more serious, we started thinking about marriage. He proposed to me, and we were married in January 2003.

We waited till the summer to go on our honeymoon, which was a cruise given to us by Darren's dad and stepmom. Neither one of us had ever been on a cruise before. As we boarded the Rhapsody of the Seas ship, we went to mass and prayed for a safe trip. This trip was one that we still talk about today. We went to play bingo after mass, and we won $349.00. We then went to e-mail his dad and stepmom to thank them for the trip and to let them know we had already won money. As I was typing the e-mail, Darren looked at the cubical next to me, and there was a man's wallet sitting there. He opened it and looked inside. The wallet was thick with $100.00 bills. He did not even want to count it as he didn't want the temptation to take it. We proceeded to the purser on the ship to find out the man's room number so we could make his day by returning his wallet with all his money in it. Needless to say, this trip became one of the best. We won several more times playing bingo. We even won a seven-day cruise for two on the last day of the cruise.

When we got home after our honeymoon and a few weeks had passed, I realized we brought home a souvenir from Grand Cayman that we would have for the rest of our lives. Yes, I was pregnant! Leah was born almost to the day nine months later, in February 2004.

Being windowed and falling in love is a tricky thing.

Something I don't think you can even begin to understand unless you have lived it.

Deciding to love again after loss was not an easy choice for me. It was brave, bold, and vulnerable. It's not easy to open up your heart that has been devastated and risk pain. With love comes loss, it's just part of the package.

Knowing I wouldn't have traded my more than fifteen years with Dennis to avoid the pain of his loss helped me open up my heart to all the time I now have with Darren.

Yes, my heart was big enough to love again, to love two men with duality. Think of it this way. When you have a second child, you don't love your first child any less, because you have a second. You love them both equally.

Deciding to open my heart to love again was incredible. Darren and I have had a few years of awful, but that is outshined by the many wonderful years we have had together. We have been married for fourteen years. We have a beautiful thirteen-year-old daughter. We also have three older children that have dealt with the grief of losing their father at such a young age. I think that Darren being a friend of Dennis helped us all a lot, as he knew the wonderful husband and father he was and understood our pain and grief, as he was grieving his friend as well.

Being widowed, you know so much more, feel so much deeper, live with more intensity, and love from a place not understood before loss.

It's not the same. It's different, unique, scary, and powerful, because you know how quickly it can be lost.

Loving with eyes wide open, knowing the frail nature of our existence, makes each moment that much more beautiful. During the first few years of my marriage with Darren, I was so in tune with the things I wish I would have shown Dennis in our fifteen years of marriage. This made me show my love and appreciation of Darren so much stronger, because I knew we did not know what tomorrow would bring.

Being widowed, you are forever changed.

You realize you only get so much time.

To understand that reality makes you feel more deeply, love more completely, and make decisions that others may consider foolish, like the years I got all leathered up and turned into a "biker chick." I got on the back of a Harley Davidson motorcycle with Darren and traveled the roads to a place I was not known as a widow.

Knowing we only get so much time has helped me to live a little bit more on the edge than I did my first thirty-six years, prewidow. It has made me more appreciative of every day I am given.

Life is in this very moment. You are guaranteed no more and no less. You have the reality of this precious moment.

Living through this made me love deeply, laugh freely, and live largely. You only get so much time. Cherish it. Live it. It's worth it, and I realize I'm still here for a reason.

Grief teaches us many things. Grief teaches perspective—love like never before, kindness, tolerance, acceptance, appreciation for the present moment, and so much more. Grief is perhaps the greatest teacher known to man, but it comes at a very steep price. I always say that I would not wish the pain of grief on my worst enemy.

Here's the tricky part When you remarry, people expect you to forget all that stuff you lived before and through—forget your ongoing grief, your children's constant grief, your memories, and your history.

You are married status now, and you can no longer identify yourself with or as a widow.

After all, loving one man completely erases your love for another. People are 100% replaceable, and because you decided to move forward with your remaining days, your choice to share your life with another voids your past history, experience, and identification with your loss. Absolutely *wrong!*

Come on folks, let's get 100% logically correct.

Nope, I'm not a widow in my current life. I'm married. My husband's name is Darren, and I hyphenate my last name to Yanchak-Fraysur. I chose to find happiness with my remaining days. I made a choice to share my lessons, my life, and my love. One does not cancel out the other. I can be both a wife to a man on this earth whom I love and the widow of a man I fulfilled my vows to until death do us part—a man I will always love.

I often have people ask me if I ever stop missing him or thinking about him, especially since I'm remarried now.

The answer is simple—no, absolutely not, and to expect me to is absolutely insane.

I don't ever stop missing him or thinking about him.

People are *not* replaceable. One person does not replace another. One love is not like another love. They are different. Love is unique.

I truly believe that great love enhances your capacity for more great love in your life. Love expands the heart. Just like having a second child, you don't love the first one any less when the second one is born.

I don't understand the people who tell me I should stop talking about my late husband. He was a part of my life for over fifteen years. He is the father of three of my children. I still grieve him even today, after seventeen years of his passing. It's of course not as intense, but there are some days it hits, and it hits hard. If you don't grieve, I believe you didn't love.

I truly believe I am to honor my past, treasure my past, and should love my past that I shared with my late husband Dennis. I believe I am to share the stories of his life so his legacy lives on through his children.

Life is messy. Love is messy. Death is messy. It comes with no instructions. There is no right or wrong in grief.

I've not been placed on this earth to fit into some mold or conform to what makes others feel comfortable with my story of loving two men passionately.

I am a wife. I am a widow. I am my own messy person who has loved and lost, grieved and grown, survived, and thrived.

I've paid the ultimate price to know who I am.

I can truly say that I am a better wife to Darren because of losing Dennis. He gets all the "I wish I would have done."

Chapter 6

Moving On

SHORTLY AFTER LEAH WAS BORN, we decided to move from Cypress, Texas, to Hempstead, Texas. I was ready to start a new chapter in my life, somewhere I wasn't known as the poor widow, hoping to leave all the grief and anger I had for God in Cypress. Well, it just doesn't happen that way.

As I started unpacking boxes into our new home, I realized I had lots of baggage I had brought with me to this new chapter of my life. I began drinking more. I would meet girlfriends at a local Mexican restaurant and have a couple margaritas at lunchtime quite often. I found myself drinking more and more as a way of numbing my grief.

As we were meeting new people in the community, most of which were parents of our now high school children, my drinking continued to increase. By this point, Darren was having a couple beers with us. We were having a great time meeting new people and made some really great friends.

We were also trail riding, and drinking is something that just goes along with that. As my older kids were starting to want to experiment with drinking, I made the decision that I would let them drink a few beers while they were with me. As they were entering high school, their desire to drink became more often. I thought I was protecting them by allowing them to have few beers at home under my supervision. There was a group of us moms that agreed to let our kids have a few beers while they were at one of our homes. We would monitor how much beer was drank and take away all their keys, and they would have to spend the night. Darren and I would be out there drinking with them.

As the next few years passed, we began drinking and partying every weekend. We would go camping, and our entire trip was planned on what alcohol was being brought and what kind of drinks we were making. We were more concerned about the alcohol than the food.

Most nights, I would go to bed early with Leah, and the next morning, I would hear the most awful stories of things that had happened after I went to bed.

This type of monitored drinking worked for most of the kids, but for my two boys and Darren, this turned into a huge problem. The drinking led to more drinking and drugs. This is where our lives began spinning out of control.

Chapter 7

One Crisis after Another

HAVE YOU EVER RIDDEN IN a helicopter? It's the ride of a lifetime! But when you land, now that's another story. A helicopter's landing sends absolutely everything flying in a hundred different directions at ridiculously high speeds. I know. This is how my life was for fourteen years.

Life is filled with crisis. Each one of us can tell our story about a disaster we have gone through or a storm we are going through now. If you are like me, you live from one crisis to another. That's just how we roll.

By this time in our life, I could see our drinking becoming a huge problem in all our lives. Darren's alcoholism was resurfacing, and I was abusing alcohol to numb my pain. The difference between the two ways we were drinking was that I could drink for a while and go to bed or not drink at all. Darren would stay up drinking all night long or drink till the cooler was empty. He also started taking hydrocodone and other drugs with his drinking. Hydrocodone was a speed to him.

My boys' drinking had now led to smoking marijuana. They were getting into trouble with the law with possession of marijuana and minor in possession of alcohol.

My older daughter was drinking too and now dating a boy I thought was in high school. I did not find out till much later that he was five years older than her and had already graduated from high school. I did not like the idea of her dating someone so much older than her, but by this time, it was too late. She was in love, and I knew if I told her she could not date him, she would go behind my back.

As her drinking continued, she started skipping school. She got into a couple of pretty serious fights in school.

Our home became the "party house" for the high school kids. The cops were called out on many occasions.

I had a storm raging around me worse than any hurricane I had ever seen. The fierceness of this storm was pounding my family for years. Storm after storm was hitting us with no breathing room in between. Looking back, I am certain, Satan had taken residency in our home.

My heart was tossed back and forth, day after day, year after year.

I'd lay awake pleading with the Lord for change, reprieve, and encouragement, not from the storms outside, but from the ones in my heart.

Perhaps my pleading was similar to what Jesus's disciples did when they were in a boat, and a windstorm suddenly came on the lake. As the boat filled with water, they wondered why Jesus continued to sleep and didn't respond to the raging storm as quickly as they wanted.

That's exactly how I felt for years. Jesus wasn't responding to my plea.

> The disciples feared the potential outcome
> of the storm. The pleaded with Jesus to help
> them, and he did, in his own time. (Luke 8:24)

I felt that same desperation that night I called for Jesus's help with a questioning heart: *Why? Why does it have to be so hard Jesus? The storms have been unrelenting.*

The question prompts me today, "Where had I been putting my trust?" The depth of my worry revealed I'd misplaced it. "When the storms rage and the winds blow, and they will, my faith needs to be in Jesus, not the outcome of my circumstances."

Today, I know that the storms will rage, and the winds will blow. But to believe in the middle of it all, to have faith that leads to hope in Jesus, that's the secret to riding out the storms of life.

At this point in my life, I was ready to make some changes. I could see the continual devastation that alcohol and drugs was causing in my family.

The hard part is that just because you are ready to make some changes, doesn't mean everyone else is ready at the same time you are.

Chapter 8

A Hunger for God's Word

*He who began a good work in you will carry it on
to completion until the day of Christ Jesus.*
—Philippians 1:6

LONG BEFORE I KNEW GOD, he knew me and loved me. I heard a whisper of God at a very young age. Having grandparents and parents who were devout in their faith truly influenced my belief in God. Through the years, I had lost that relationship with him through loss and grief, my trust in God became questionable.

For twelve years, after the loss of my husband and my mother, I was looking everywhere to fill that hole in my heart.

I had turned to drinking and partying, but now after seeing the devastation it was causing me and my family, I was ready for change. I craved something more than fun and diversion, more than a life of partying. But what? Looking back, I see my inner hunger drove me for ways to find myself again, but none of them worked.

My soul hungered for something more.

I saw my family falling apart long before I made some changes in me. I would pray for happiness and changes. I started withdrawing from the crowd we were running with. I would take my own car, so when Darren's drinking would get out of hand, I could leave.

Daily, I began to keep a journal, pray, and read Bible verses—something I used to do seventeen years ago, when my life was at the best it had ever been prior to this time in my life. As I did, I felt a deep awakening in my heart, and power was flowing into me.

As more storms hit our family, I would start to panic about our crazy life. My first instinct kicked in. Suddenly, I stopped and prayed, for my family and for this craziness to end and for peace, for us all.

I talked to Darren about going back to church. We had visited many churches through our marriage but had not found one to call home. It was hard for us to find one that we both liked. With my Catholic upbringing, it was hard for us to find a church. He was not brought up Catholic and did not feel comfortable in the Catholic Church. So once again, we started church hopping. We found one in Hockley that we liked and would go occasionally.

With me still holding on to my grief and anger, no matter what church we went into, I was just going through the motions. I would pray, but still wasn't seeing my prayers being answered. I know today that was because of the anger I was holding on to.

We continued to go to this church for several years. The message was always good, and we both loved this church. But I still wasn't finding the peace I wanted, and my prayers weren't being answered the way I thought they should.

While my drinking had slowed down tremendously, Darren's was getting worse. He started bringing home cases of beer a lot after work during the week and drinking alone.

The boys at this time were working on the pipeline, and when they would come home, Darren would go with them to the neighborhood bar. At this point, Darren knew his drinking was getting out of hand, as he had a wrecker driver on standby that would come to the bar at closing time, tap him on the shoulder, and tell him, "Your truck is loaded up and ready to go." The wrecker driver would then drive Darren home with his truck in tow.

Chapter 9

When Life Is Too Much to Bear

I NEVER UNDERSTOOD WHAT IT meant to get to the end of yourself, until I reached this point in my life. I was facing situations beyond my abilities, situations that I truly believe were not part of God's plan. These situations were caused by poor choices made by so many people in my life. I had also made plenty of poor choices in my life, but I was ready to make some changes. I was also making very poor choices as I tried to take control and change everyone else with me. I tried to take control by trying to fix things and people myself. This plan was not working at all. I needed the Lord, and I needed him desperately. My desperation took me to a new dependence on God. If the Lord didn't sustain me, my heart felt like it would crumble to pieces. I started to feel some peace at this point.

A big part of that peace and trust in Jesus came from my faith. Faith came from looking back at my life after Dennis died and how well God took care of me and my children. I didn't know how or when, but I knew God would answer my prayers for my family. Patience is not my greatest attribute, so this was extremely difficult for me. But I kept praying.

I realized it wasn't up to me to "fix" people or the situation— that was God's job. He guided me every step of the way for *his* plan. I was to be part of the journey with God.

As a young believer, I'd heard testimonies of God working and showing up when he was most needed.

Sometimes, we don't experience God, because we simply don't need Him or so we think. When life is firmly under our control, we operate in our strength. But when life is falling apart, our deep need opens our eyes. In our darkest times, we see God's power, feel His presence, and experience his peace. This is what was slowly happening to me.

Chapter 10

Waiting on God for Answered Prayer

*The Lord is good to those who wait hopefully and
expectantly for Him, to those who seek Him.*

—Lamentations 3:25

SOMETIMES, I SEE GOD ANSWER my prayers right away. I'm excited, thankful, and ready to tell everyone about his goodness. Then there are those other times when my prayers linger and answers seem far away. As time creeps on, my doubts creep in.

Yet, while I lost days and emotions within the great frustration, I still pushed on.

So, with my wait on my mind, I can't help but ask God this question: "God, why do you send us through waiting that feels excruciating?"

I began to think God might be holding out on me. Maybe he really didn't care about me. Or, maybe my circumstances weren't important enough to him.

But as I grew in my relationship with the Lord and learned to understand his character, my attitude changed. I realized how much God loves me and knows the desires tucked deep inside my heart. He promises to meet my needs (Philippians 4:19), and his miracles are not a thing of the past.

I have learned that sometimes, my prayers aren't answered right away because God is working behind the scenes, getting everything

43

to line up, to get everything to work out perfectly. *His* perfect answer to my prayer. Sometimes the answer to my prayer takes longer because it requires changing the actions of other people. This is hard for an impatient person, who likes to see changes *now*. But learning patience was also an attribute God wanted me to possess.

The following three verses bring clarity:

> Our light and momentary troubles are achieving for us an eternal glory that far outweighs them all. (2 Corinthians 4:17)

Our investment in waiting today is deposited in heaven for tomorrow. This eternal glory exceeds anything we could want in the here and now.

> Wait for the *Lord*; be strong and take heart and wait for the *Lord*. (Psalm 27:14)

We can choose to be strong, because, during times of wait, we have faith. Faith is activated when we remember God is always at work (John 5:17), he won't leave us, and he loves us.

> Consider it pure joy, my brothers and sisters, whenever you face trials of many kinds, because you know that the testing of your faith produces perseverance. (James 1:2)

Just as a runner trains for a big race, so do trials train us for the most important race of our life. Trials give us the mindsets, and the perseverance to tackle God's greatest missions. They, although difficult in the moment, prepare us for wildly important kingdom work.

Wherever you stand—or sit around waiting—today, know this: Your good God has good plans for you. He has not disowned you. He has not turned his back from you. He loves you and is near. He is working behind the scenes. Take heart and wait for the Lord.

Today's key verse tells us that after we pray and ask God for a need, want, or desire, we should wait with expectancy and hope.

You might be thinking, *You just don't understand. I've been waiting for God to answer my prayers for so long.*

Maybe you've resigned to believing there's no hope. Sure, you started out confident and faith-filled, but as time goes by, you've started to wonder if any good can come from your circumstances.

Maybe you've wrapped an invisible wall around your heart so you won't be disappointed if God doesn't come through for you.

Friend, I understand. I've been there. I've felt that way, too, and it's a lonely place to live each day.

So what does it look like to have an attitude of hope and expectancy as we wait on the Lord to answer our prayers?

I've learned to intentionally shift my focus to the following three things:

God's promises: I read Bible verses and speak them aloud daily. As the power of God's Word weaves hope into my prayers, encouragement fills the empty places in my heart. I'm reminded once again of God's unfailing love and faithfulness.

Praise and worship: I listen to praise music throughout the day in my house, car, and outside by the pool. The lyrics and melodies splash over me with joy as I sing along. I sense God's peace and pleasure, and in those sweet moments, my worries fade, turning my doubts into confident expectancy.

Thanksgiving: I thank God for the answered prayers and restoration in my life. I remember how God always came through in those tough times of great need, and I thank him in advance for his answers yet to come.

If you've asked God for answers but find yourself waiting longer than you planned, take a moment now to thank him in advance for his answer. Trust that he is working behind the scenes on your behalf. Don't give up. Look forward in hope and expectancy for him to respond and remember that the Lord is good to those who seek him.

Sometimes, it does seem like our prayers are just bouncing off the ceiling. But what we feel isn't always the same as what's really true.

The Bible teaches us that God does answer our prayers (John 16:24). But there are a few things we have to remember: God's answer may not always be what we were hoping for. His answer sometimes is simply "no." And his answer might be something we'll never completely understand. In any case, his answer is always the best answer. He loves us dearly, and his answers to our prayers are always what we need, even if they're not necessarily what we want.

Yes, prayer is a time to be honest with God about what we want. But it's also a time for us to recognize who's really in control. And it's a time to ask God to help us understand—and accept—what he brings to our lives.

The bottom line: As Christians, we need to put God first in our lives to have an effective prayer life. If you're doing that, God does hear your prayers, and he answers them.

You just have to trust God that he's giving you the best answer for you, for your life, and for all eternity: "Trust in the Lord with all your heart and lean not on your own understanding; in all your ways acknowledge him, and he will make your paths straight" (Proverbs 3:5–6).

Chapter 11

I Just Want to Run—
Run as Fast as I Can

*From the ends of the Earth, I cry to you for help when my heart
is overwhelmed. Lead me to the towering rock of safety.*
—Psalm 61:2

IN JULY 2013, I WENT on a short vacation with Leah, my sister, her
two children, and one of my best friends, Linda.

We went to Galveston, to stay a few days, get away, and have a
nice little retreat. Our first day there, I went to the grocery store with
Leah and slipped and fell. I cracked my hip, twisted my ankle, and
injured my back and neck.

Needless to say, our trip was cut short, and we headed back the
next morning. I was not able to drive my car from the pain in my hip
and back. When we got back home, I went to the ER and had some
x-rays and MRIs done that showed I had bulging disks in my back
and neck. As the days went by, I was starting to feel some numbness
in my arms and legs. By day twenty-eight, I had lost continence and
had gone paralyzed from the neck down.

I had my good friend, Marna, take me to the hospital, as Darren
was busy working on a project. Once I got to the hospital, the doctor
on call had them do another MRI, this time one with contrast. This
MRI showed that I was losing spinal fluid from the injury sustained
from the fall in my cervical spine. The doctor told me and my family

that he had to do surgery immediately, as I would not live another week without it. I went into surgery the next day, where they put a plate and eight screws at C4–C7.

As soon as the surgery was over, I had regained all feeling I had lost in my body. I still had some nerve damage that would take time to heal. The doctor told me it could take up to eighteen months to fully regain all the feeling back 100 percent. I suffered from a lot of neuropathy in my arms and legs. I was prescribed more medicine than should be legal. I have an extremely low tolerance to medication to begin with. On the amount of medication I was prescribed, I could not function. I slept a lot, for the next couple months.

I still had several health issues, and we were trying to figure out why. My friend Marna, who was taking as good of care of me as my own mother, was taking me to my many doctor visits. They were doing more MRIs to see if the fusion in my neck was healing properly and trying to figure out why I was having so many other health issues surfacing. In doing the MRIs, they would give me valium to take so I could withstand being in the MRI machine. There was one point where they were needing to do an MRI on my neck and my back. They did the back first. After lying in the MRI machine for almost an hour, I could no longer lay there to do the MRI on my neck, as the pain in my back was intolerable. They sent me home with another prescription of valium to take the next morning before the MRI on my neck.

I woke up the next morning, took my regular prescriptions for pain and neuropathy, plus a second valium in two days. I drove my daughter to school and met Marna in Waller for breakfast, where I left my car and rode with her to get the MRI on my neck. I also had a follow-up appointment with the surgeon that did my neck surgery to discuss the new health issues I was having. In the restaurant, I literally passed out. Marna somehow got me into the car, and by the time, we got to the hospital to do the MRI, I was totally unresponsive. She got me into a wheelchair and took me straight to the surgeon's office, as she did not know what else to do. The nurse there told her to take me downstairs to the ER. They checked me into the ER and hooked me up to an IV to get fluids in me to flush the meds out of my body. I have absolutely no recollection from the time I left my home that morning to coming home. I slept the entire weekend. I was so overmedicated that I don't even remember my sister Debbie and her friend Deb coming over to check on me. They were counting my pills in my bottle, calling the pharmacy to see if I had taken more medication than I was prescribed. The bottom line, I was totally overmedicated.

The next Monday morning, my sister Carolyn came to go with me to the appointment I had with my new pain management doctor. We took all my prescriptions with us. He looked at all the prescriptions I had been prescribed and was amazed that I was functioning at all. I was prescribed gabapentin for neuropathy. The dosage prescribed to me was for a 350-pound man.

At this point, I wanted to get off all medication, as I was so scared. I went to my sister Carolyn's home and detoxed off everything I was prescribed, cold turkey. The gabapentin, so I read when I researched it, was like getting off heroine. It is actually called the drug of Satan, which I totally agree with. Getting off all that medicine took a week, and the detox was an absolute nightmare.

By this time in our lives, Darren was still drinking heavily and was now stealing my hydrocodone. I had to hide it. There were days he would beg me for hydrocodone. I just didn't understand why someone would want hydrocodone for no reason. It made me very tired, and all I wanted to do was sleep. But to Darren's body, the hydrocodone was a form of speed.

He was sleeping in a guest bedroom in our home. I had no idea what he was doing day in and day out. I had no idea what time he was going to bed or what time he was waking up. He was living his own private life. I was trying to recuperate from the fall I had taken, the neck surgery, and my herniated disks in my back. He also had a family member who had recently been in jail for a year, for distribution, manufacturing, and selling meth, who stayed with us in our guest house.

At this point, things really got crazy. I would wake up in the middle of the night to some really scary, questionable people in my home—in our game room, in my den, and in my kitchen. These people were so scary-looking to me. I have never seen these types of people during daylight. That's for sure. My home started looking like something from *Criminal Minds*.

It wasn't long that Leah and a friend of hers found some meth and a crack pipe in our guest house, where Darren's family member was staying. I had Darren confront this family member and told Darren he needed to leave immediately. Darren did not make this person leave. The longer he stayed, the madder I got. I would try to explain to Darren that if Leah's friend's mother wanted to call CPS, we would lose Leah. This didn't seem to bother Darren, and he wasn't too concerned. I just kept getting madder and madder, as the days went by.

One day, I decided to go into the guest house while Darren and this family member were gone. I don't know what I was looking for, but I was hoping to find something. The door was locked, which really set me off. How dare he lock me out of my guest house! I found an open window and crawled in. I looked through everything in the closet and in the bathroom cabinets. I went to the nightstand and searched it. As I looked at the bed, I thought, *Under the mattress!* As I went to lift the mattress, something moved on the bed. I looked up, and there was a person lying in the bed. It startled me, and I screamed, "Who the h—— are you, and what are you doing in my home?" She said that she was a friend of the family member of Darren's, who was staying in the guest house. I told her that she needed to leave immediately, or I would call the police.

She said, "I don't have a ride."

I said, "You have two feet. Start walking." I then went back into the house, called Darren, and told him that he had one hour to get the family member and this woman out of my home or I would call the police and tell them to bring drug dogs.

When Darren and his family member got back to the house, his family member packed up his stuff and, before leaving with that woman, told me if I didn't keep my mouth shut about the meth, he would have me killed. Darren heard this threat and said nothing.

Darren and I went to see a counselor at the church we were attending and took Leah to one there as well. We all went to counseling for several months, but things were not getting any better, and Darren's attitude toward me at this time was getting worse. He was verbally and mentally very abusive. I think he realized I was on to him. I did not know how or what to do or how to handle the situation, but I wanted to know if he was using meth. My gut told me that he was, and I had been suspecting it for a while.

As I said before, God was leading me one day at a time, one step at a time. I heard God tell me to go get a drug test and ask Darren to take it. So I did.

When I brought the drug test home and asked Darren to take it, he refused. I told him that his refusing to take the test was confirmation to me that he was using meth. He still refused.

Chapter 12

Wisdom for the Trials We Face in Life

WHY DOES GOD ALLOW US to go through hard times? Sometimes, Christians assume that if they're following the Lord, he should protect them from problems. But Jesus never promised his disciples' lives as ease and comfort. On the contrary, he told them to expect tribulation (John 16:33). After all, Christ himself wasn't exempt from afflictions. He was called "a man of sorrows" (Isaiah 53:3).

Trials have been the common experience of mankind throughout history. By looking back on such situations from God's perspective, we can gain insight that will help us respond wisely in the future. The Lord uses hardships to achieve something good in our lives, but whether we experience these benefits depends on our response.

Develop the Right Attitude

What is your behavior when experiencing difficulty or pain? Do you grumble and complain or indulge in self-pity? Or do you get angry and blame others for your troubles? All these reactions lead to despair and misery, but James 1:2–6 presents a totally different perspective about suffering: "Consider it all joy, my brethren, when you encounter various trials" (v. 2).

Some may read that verse and think, *What a preposterous statement!* Trials and tears go together. How is joy possible? Yet James obviously understands something about suffering that we need to know. The word consider is a financial term that means "to evaluate." James isn't telling us to delight in pain and be happy about suffering, but to assess our trials as an opportunity to receive the blessings God has promised us when we respond wisely.

I don't know what you're facing right now. But I do know that if you're willing to count it as joy, you will find God's goodness right in the middle of suffering. Unlike happiness, joy is not dependent upon pleasant circumstances, because it's produced by the indwelling Holy Spirit.

Determine the Source

Have you ever noticed that troubles come in all shapes and sizes? They also tend to pop up unexpectedly and sometimes one right after another. In fact, you may feel as if you're dealing with an entire range of difficulties.

Knowing how a trial began can help you understand the wise way to react. Since our problems originate from different sources, we need to adapt our responses accordingly. Each time you encounter difficulty, ask the Lord to help you determine the cause and the proper response. Here are some common sources of hardship:

Self. Sometimes, we get ourselves in trouble with our own choices or actions. We may find ourselves standing in a field of trials simply because we've planted troublesome seed and are now reaping what we've sown (Galatians 6:7–8). The good news is that if we'll repent and humble ourselves, the Lord will redeem our failures and teach us valuable lessons.

Others. But there are also times when our problems result from someone else's decisions or conduct. Perhaps a loved one's behavior has caused you suffering, or maybe an enemy is maliciously accusing and maligning you. Either way, the pain is real. Your job is to forgive those who wrong you, guard against resentment, and seek God's wisdom in dealing with the situation in a way that honors him.

World. Many of our trials are simply the result of living in a fallen world—accidents happen, people get sick, natural disasters strike, and wars erupt. And we have no control over any of it. Our hope is that one day when Christ returns, all this will end—we'll finally live at peace. In the meantime, drawing on the sustaining power of the Holy Spirit will enable us to respond in a manner that draws others to the Savior.

Satan. We also have an *adversary* who wants to devour us. The devil is constantly working against us to weaken our faith, ruin our testimony, and make us useless in the kingdom of God. But we're not helpless against his onslaught. The Father has given us his spiritual armor to protect us from enemy attacks (Ephesians 6:11).

God. Because the Lord is sovereign over all things, no trial can touch us unless he has first allowed it to do so. Our heavenly Father knows that sometimes, the only way we'll grow spiritually is through suffering. Pain can sharpen our sensitivity to his presence and give us ears to hear when we have been deaf to his voice. It reveals hidden sins and purifies us the way fire refines gold. From a human perspective, trials hurt; but from God's viewpoint, they are a bridge to a deeper relationship with him.

Understand God's purposes. Meaningless suffering is exhausting and demoralizing, but if we understand that there is a purpose and a benefit to our troubles, we can endure just about anything. The reason James could rejoice in trials was because he knew God was achieving something good. Though we may not know his specific purpose for each individual challenge or obstacle, scripture reveals his overall goals.

The testing of your faith. For faith to be genuine, it must be tested—just as weightlifters rely on resistance to make their muscles stronger. When everything's going well, it is easy to say, "Sure, I trust the Lord." But when times get tough, confidence in him can take a nosedive. Will you believe and act on the truths in the scripture or let hardship cause you to doubt his love and care for you? Each moment of adversity you face is an opportunity to believe God, rest in his promises, and grow further into his likeness.

Produces endurance. One of the most valuable qualities the Lord desires to produce in our life is endurance. That may not be what we desire when suffering knocks on our door. But the Lord knows that some lessons are learned only under the pressure of adversity. Yet even then, he sovereignly and lovingly protects us by determining the length and intensity of each trial. Although we may think we can't endure it, he knows our limits and will not go beyond them.

The kind of endurance God wants for us is not resignation in which we grumble, saying, "Well, I can't do anything to change my situation, so I guess I'm stuck with it." His goal is that we patiently abide the trial with an attitude of unfailing trust in his goodness and complete reliance upon his strength. The only way we can do this is to have a firm determination to live for his purposes, regardless of the cost.

That you may be perfect and complete. James tells us that to endure hardships in this way will have amazing results—but not that we're going to be sinless. "Perfect and complete" means that we will be mature and fully developed. Being born again is not the end goal in the Christian life; it's just the beginning. From that point on, God wants us to grow up to become mature men and women of faith. His goal is to conform us to the image of his Son (Romans 8:29), and trials play a vital role in this lifelong process. He uses them to sand away ungodly qualities, sift out sinful habits and attitudes, and polish our character until we reflect Christ.

Lacking in nothing. Perhaps the most surprising benefit of trials is that they supply something we need. If you endure hardship with the right attitude, James says you'll come out "lacking in nothing" (1:4). The Apostle Paul said that his "thorn in the flesh" was given to teach him humility and dependence on Christ (2 Corinthians 12:7–10). But he also says that the Lord comforted him in his afflictions so that he'd be able to comfort others (1:3–4). If you want to become useful in God's kingdom, brokenness is the path the Lord uses to produce the qualities needed to accomplish His will.

Cooperate with God's Goals

Although all of these benefits are available to you, they are not automatically yours. But by following James's commands in these few verses, we open ourselves up to God's promised blessings—all the tools we need to live victoriously in him. So consider trials an occasion for joy and let endurance produce its fruit, because then your suffering will be profitable, both now and in eternity. If you lack wisdom in responding to trials, the Lord invites you to ask him for it and in faith expect to receive (James 1:5–6).

The crown of life awaits those who persevere under trial and are approved (1:12). God wants to do great things in you—and he will, if you'll let him. But he won't force any of this upon you. The choice is yours. Won't you allow him to use adversity to transform you?

Chapter 13

Stress

*The Lord is my strength and shield. I trust him with
all my heart. He helps me, and my heart is filled
with joy. I burst out in songs of thanksgiving.*

—Psalm 28:7

*The Lord gives strength to his people; the
Lord blesses his people with peace.*

—Psalm 29:11

AMERICANS ARE MORE STRESSED THAN ever, according to an American
Psychological Association survey, and nearly one-third say stress
impacts their physical or mental health.

I was suddenly covered, from head to toe, with itchy red bumps;
stress (not allergies) were to blame. When your body experiences
excessive stress (for a long period of time), your immune system goes
crazy, and your body starts releasing the chemical histamine to fight
off your ailment. If the stress doesn't go away, you essentially develop
an allergic reaction, and boom, hives galore. Yes, your body becomes
literally allergic to stress, inside and out. When your immune system
is weakened by stress, your skin, lungs, heart, thyroid, etc., all get
affected; it is a vicious cycle.

Through the years, I have realized that I can no longer handle
stress at all. I was diagnosed with nine autoimmune diseases while I

was going through my separation with Darren. These autoimmune diseases were affecting my thyroid, skin, heart, and lungs. My doctor said that these autoimmune diseases were activated by stress. He also said that if I didn't get a handle on my stress, these autoimmune diseases would eventually kill me. My stress level was definitely at an all-time record level. I seriously don't think I could have taken anymore. Truth be known, when I look back, I probably had a nervous breakdown. My life couldn't get any more stressful.

After the past three years of doing Bible studies, I learned how to cure stress, "let go and let God," as they say. But to be able to "let go and let God," I needed to be in God's Word every day. I needed to know what God's Word says and how to "let go and let God."

God's strength shields us from the fiery darts of worry, fear, and stress.

I have learned that "if I have stress, that means I'm not trusting God."

In John 16:33, God tells us, "I have told you these things, so that in me you may have peace. In this world you will have trouble. But take heart! I have overcome the world." God also tells us how to have peace when trouble comes throughout the Bible.

Today, when I feel my stress level rise, with sweat trickling between my shoulder blades, heart racing, hard time breathing, and feeling all flush, I know there is a way to deal with the stress other than on my own.

I have learned how to live my life in a deeper relationship with God. Living in this fallen world, we will have days of stress.

But now, I have to laugh at myself for not including more of God in my day, when I get stressed. Sure, I shout off many help-me-Lord prayers in the moment. But I now know I need to do more than the shout out, "Help me, Lord."

When you get stressed, I suggest unpacking Psalm 28:7.

This verse starts with "The *Lord* is my strength and shield."

This is a great reminder that we can use God's strength to make it through any of our problems. In fact, God's strength can serve to shield us from the fiery darts of worry, fear, and stress. This news is a great relief!

The next line of this verse says, "I trust him with all my heart."

These words prompt us to trust God. The next time you're tempted to turn a hectic day into a panic attack, instead say, "I'm going to trust God through this." You'll soon discover that your choice to trust God will calm you with a peace that surpasses understanding.

The rest of the verse says, "He helps me, and my heart is filled with joy. I burst out in songs of thanksgiving."

This puts us on notice to acknowledge God's help and presence in our lives. When we take the time to count our blessings, to remind ourselves of all the ways God has helped us through difficulties, we are sure to experience his joy.

When we remember to trust God and to face stress in his strength, we'll see our blessings and count it all as joy.

I have finally figured out I need God's help every day to deal with all my stress. Life will always have stress. God will help me calm down and get a grip on my life and keep me from getting sick.

No matter how stressful my life gets, I know I can handle it with help from God.

Chapter 14

Listening for God's Command, One Step at a Time

Trust in the Lord with all your heart and lean not on your own understanding; in all your ways acknowledge him, and he will make your paths straight.
—Proverbs 3:5–6

WHEN YOU FEEL LIKE GIVING up, take one step at a time, listening for God's command for the next step

I felt like I was facing a dead end. God could see a path that I couldn't see. I trusted God and kept on moving in faith. Even when I didn't see a way, he made a way. I just took one step at a time, listening to the Holy Spirit, as he guided my next step.

When my life took that wild and crazy turn, I thought I had problems that were bigger than anything even God could fix.

In my desperation, I didn't just pray—I cried to the Lord. I needed more than another sermon illustration, more than a checklist of dos and don'ts. I really needed to know that not only was God near, but also he would get me through this. But how?

I began praying, praying for the strength to uncover what I knew was going on in my home.

> For who is God, but the *Lord*? And who is a
> rock, except our God?—the God who equipped
> me with strength. (Psalm 18:31–32)

As I meditated on these verses, the phrase "who equipped me with strength" captured my attention. I found myself begging. *Lord, I need the kind of strength only you can give. I need this equipping process, Jesus. Will you please help me?*

It was time for me to make some drastic changes in my life. I could no longer live the way I was in my marriage and in my home. My home became a very scary place to live with some very scary people hanging around there. Drugs had taken over. I would wake up in the middle of the night with what looked like scenes from *Criminal Minds*.

The Holy Spirit prompted me through this reflection in Psalms. I heard God, loud and clear, tell me that it was time to leave. That's it! That's what I need to do!

When I feel like giving up, I don't have to comprehend the entire journey. I only need enough strength to take that first step and then stop and listen for my next step.

I can take comfort in the fact that God's plan is always bigger and better than mine.

Echoing the words of the psalmist, I whispered to God that the battle felt enormously overwhelming. I asked him to equip me with strength only he can give (Psalm 18:39)

God's power and provision would carry me through whatever came my way that day I would leave with Leah.

Have you felt like giving up lately? Let's stop thinking about the vastness of the journey. Let's recognize that when things seem out of control, God is always in control. He is with us and giving us the strength to take one more step.

I can take comfort in knowing that God's plans are bigger and better than mine! Sometimes, he has to take us through those deep dark valleys to get us totally dependent on him for our next step!

It became more understandable as I headed down the path he set before me, but understanding is not a requirement for you to start down the path. Proverbs 4:18 says, "The path of the righteous is like the first gleam of dawn, shining brighter till the full light of day." One day, you will stand in the full view of the big picture. You'll see God's purpose behind the path he specifically chose for you.

What do I do in the meantime? You do what Proverbs 3 says: "Trust in the Lord with all your heart and lean not on your own understanding; in all your ways acknowledge him, and he will make your paths straight." What does he mean "don't lean on your own understanding"? You don't need to try to figure it all out. In truth, you're not going to understand most of the things that happen in your life until years later and some not till you get to heaven.

Be patient. God knows what he's doing. God knows what's best for you. He can see the end result. You can't. All those problems, heartaches, difficulties, and delays—all the things that make you ask "why"—one day, it will all be clear in the light of God's love.

But for now, we're learning to trust God.

I started hearing God telling me to leave. But how can that be? God doesn't believe in divorce. I was raised Catholic, and that definitely went against anything I was taught. So I questioned what I was hearing.

Chapter 15

God's Purpose for Us
Going through Trials

Dear friends, do not be surprised at the fiery ordeal that has come on you to test you, as though something strange were happening to you. But rejoice inasmuch as you participate in the sufferings of Christ, so that you may be overjoyed when his glory is revealed.
—1 Peter 4:12–13

SOME BELIEVERS LIKE TO PORTRAY their lives as ideal and carefree. But in reality, being a Christian isn't always easy. In fact, sometimes, we'll experience trials that truly test our faith and ability to trust in God.

In today's passage, Peter refers to times of testing as "fiery ordeals." He says that we shouldn't be surprised when adversity comes our way. It's important to remember that God has a purpose for our trials and will see us through each step of the way. But what purpose does God have for the hardships we face?

First, the heavenly Father will sometimes use painful experiences to cleanse and purify his children's lives. Trials drive us to the Lord. Then, as we begin to focus on him, we're increasingl to see things from his perspective and often become more our sin.

Second, the Lord at times allows difficulty in our li of testing us—he might be trying our faith, enduranc to him. He uses such experiences to reveal something about our spiritual development and to strengthen our faith.

Third, God uses suffering to demonstrate his power to sustain us. When he brings us through difficult times, he glorifies himself. In turn, this encourages others when they experience trials, because they have witnessed God's sustaining power in our lives.

When I look back on my life, I see the many trials I have been through and wonder how I'm still standing to talk about them. Sometimes, it felt like I just couldn't catch a break—From death of loved ones, to family members making poor choices, to an almost divorce, to being threatened by a drug dealer, to having someone point a gun at me and threaten to kill me, and not to mention my own poor choices that caused me lots of grief. When I look back on the trials I have been through, I can tell you the years I quit going to church, quit doing Bible studies, and quit praying, I wasn't hearing from the Holy Spirit. It was during those years of my life that the trials were so much harder and so much more painful. I know now that it was because I wasn't relying on Jesus to get me through, to comfort me, or to give me the guidance I desperately needed.

For the last three years, I have been finding my way back to Jesus. I have been faithfully going to church, doing Bible studies, leaning on Jesus during those hard times, and listening to the Holy Spirit. I still have trials and hard times, but the trials and hard times I have had to face the past three years have been so much easier for me to deal with. I have gotten through them without looking and feeling like a crazy woman, because I now have Jesus back in my life, guiding me and giving me the strength I need. I am no longer trying to handle these trials and hard times *on my own*. When I compare my life with Jesus and without Jesus, I can tell you I most certainly *never* want to go back where I was just five years ago. I know I can't handle my life and the trials I face without Jesus.

God is speaking his own Word to me today,

> Consider it pure joy, my brothers and sisters, whenever you face trials of many kinds, because you know that the testing of your faith

produces perseverance. Let perseverance finish its
work so that you may be mature and complete,
not lacking anything. (James 1:2–4)

Sometimes, God allows trials to test our faith. Our trials, though incredibly confusing and painful, initiate a process that teaches perseverance that deepens and matures our faith in a way nothing else can.

My life is proof. Not only has God healed me from those horrific days from years ago, but also he has turned it into a powerful testimony to bring hope to others and point them to him.

If you're in the midst of a trial, be encouraged, sweet friend. These key verses teach that God promises to mature and complete you through it. He also promises that you will be more than a conqueror through Christ who loves you. Pay attention to those words—not a mere conqueror, but more than a conqueror (Romans 8:37).

As God washed these truths over me, he spoke this message into my heart,

"Not only can these trials not separate you from me, Tessie, but with me, if you continue to look to me and trust me, I will use it to mold you into the woman I created you to be. Tessie, you will be more than a conqueror so that I can mature you and use you to encourage and help others."

Before you read further, reread the paragraph above and replace my name with yours. Let God's promises seep deep into your heart. Your trial has purpose. It forces dependence on God. It tests you. It molds you, eventually creating you into an overcomer, with a powerful testimony.

Ultimately, hardships strengthen our testimony. In the midst of our struggles, we might feel overwhelmed. But once the storm has passed, we can often look back and see the Lord's providential hand carrying us through.

Trials come so that God can work in and through them to transform us and then use us to bring hope and healing to his hurting people.

Heavenly Father, thank you for having a purpose in my trials. Open my eyes to see your hand at work and give me the courage to persevere so that you can mold me into the woman you created me to be.

Chapter 16

Living with an Addict

Don't worry about anything, but pray about everything.
—Philippians 4:6

"A CODEPENDENT PERSON IS ONE who has let another person's behavior affect him or her and who is obsessed with controlling that person's behavior."

If we are being perfectly honest, there comes a time where loving and doing for an addict becomes so maddening and demanding that we secretly wonder if it's actually worth it. In our own lowest personal moments, we stop trying to help out of love and begin acting out of a desperate need to control the other person's behavior.

Think about the insane position we put ourselves in—we try to control the (often irrational) actions of an addict. And since the addict's actions are ruled by his or her addiction, let's put this in an even more crazy perspective—we try to control someone else's addiction.

We are doomed to fail at this because we are acting out of ignorance, fear, or both.

It starts out as a genuine desire to help a loved one who is addicted to drugs or alcohol, but it inevitably deteriorates into resentment at the lack of appreciation, reciprocation, or progress on the part of the addict.

Our Own Insanity

We may even begin to "act out" ourselves, in ways an outsider would think, well, crazy. Does any of this sound familiar? I know I thought I was losing my mind and was acting very crazy during this time in my life as I did not understand the disease.

Blaming the addict. Would you blame any other sick person for their disease?

Trying to micromanage their money. Do you expect an addict to be honest about money?

Keeping tabs on their every movement, every minute. Are you trying to keep up with their schedule *and* your own?

Taking time off from work or other obligations to drive around looking for them. What are you going to do when you find them?

Checking whatever you can find—their phone, texts, wallet, purse, pockets, car, room, etc. Do you even know what you are looking for?

The endless arguments, begging, pleading, threats, and broken promises. Has this ever gotten you anywhere? If not, why do you keep doing it?

As the old saying goes, "The definition of insanity is doing the same thing over and over yet expecting different results."

Your Own Problem

All of these things you are doing are not changing the addict's behavior at all, yet you are going crazy. Obsessing over what the addict is doing is making you angry and bitter, because you are losing focus when it comes to your own life.

You are powerless over the drug/alcohol, and your life has become unmanageable due to substance abuse. Ironically, that is nearly word for word the first step of the 12 Steps that serve as the foundation for so many recovery programs.

Because that statement fits you so well, it indicates that you too have a problem. The problem isn't necessarily that you are abusing alcohol or drugs. The problem is that you are letting your loved one's addiction destroy your life as well.

It doesn't matter if you are only trying to help. If you are sick and damaged yourself, and if you are acting just as irrationally as the addict, then you have nothing of value to offer them, in terms of a healthy recovery from addiction.

What You *Can Do*

In your damaged condition, you are doing nothing at all to help the addict. Every effort you are making is at best slowing the disease's progress, but it will not motivate a true recovery effort.

Your time and energy would be better utilized focusing on you. Although you cannot control what the addict is doing, you can control yourself and how much impact their addiction has on your life.

Focus on your own recovery. Take it one day at a time, step by step, as you navigate the mental, emotional, and physical demands of dealing with someone else's addiction.

Set personal boundaries. Adopt strict limits as to how much you will allow the addict and their behavior to impact other areas of your life and stick to them.

Set aside quiet time. Every day, take some time to pray, while you set aside your problems. It doesn't have to be long, even fifteen minutes a day will give you a chance to recharge your batteries and hear from God.

Get outside help. Having an addict in your life is one of the most stressful things that could ever happen to you, and there is no sense trying to go it alone. Talk to trained professionals who specialize in addiction-related counseling for families, even if you have to go alone.

Join a support group. Despite how you might have been feeling, you are not alone in your struggle. When you share your problems within a group fellowship, you will find a measure of comfort that you never thought possible.

Of course, it will always be your loving wish that the addict in your life gets the help they need and is able to return to a serene life of sobriety, but ultimately, their recovery will depend upon them.

If you adopt the same mindset—that your personal Lasting Recovery from insane codependency is completely up to you—you will regain serenity and sanity no matter what the addict does.

If you or someone you are close to is struggling with drug or alcohol addiction, make the call to Lasting Recovery today—you *can* restore stability, sanity, and sobriety to your life, Lasting Recovery— "Where Wellness Begins ..."

My husband was addicted to meth and alcohol. For years, this reality shattered my world.

Watching someone you love in the throes of an addiction can be devastating. I watched my husband struggle with alcoholism and drug abuse for years, though I've come to realize that he wasn't the only one battling the addiction—I was living the struggle with him. And it doesn't just affect me; it affects everyone. It affected how we come together as a family, it affected his business, and it affected our children. We were all on this painful journey with him. But we are not bystanders. The Bible says in Philippians 4:6, "Don't worry about anything, but pray about everything." Pray, because God hears us when we pray—and he has the power to change lives!

Maybe you are feeling pain and anguish. I did because someone you love is struggling with an addiction. Whether it is alcohol, drugs, pornography, or something else, you don't have to stand by and watch your loved one suffer. You are not powerless in this situation, because God wants you to come to him with the struggles that cause you pain. Here are three Bible verses you can pray when supporting a loved one battling an addiction:

> Pray for your loved one's brokenness and emptiness. He heals the broken-hearted and bandages their wounds. (Psalm 147:3)
>
> Pray for your loved ones' freedom and deliverance. If the Son sets you free, then you will be really free. (John 8:36)

Turn to God, resist the devil, and he shall
flee (James 4:7)

Pray for your loved one's restoration.

Anyone who is joined to Christ is a new being; the old is gone;
the new has come.

Chapter 17

The Day I Gave Up and
Gave It All to God

*The eyes of the Lord are on the righteous, and His ears are
open to their cry for help. The righteous cry out, and the Lord
hears, and delivers them from all their troubles. The Lord is
near the brokenhearted; He saves those crushed in spirit."*
—Psalm 34:15–18

I COULD NOT TAKE ANYMORE. I think I was literally having a nervous
breakdown. My heart pounded furiously, like a time bomb waiting
to explode. The pressure in my head was almost unbearable. The
invisible weight on my chest felt like someone dropped a sledgeham-
mer on me. I was covered in the most awful itchy rash from head to
toe. My thyroid was swollen twice its size. I could hardly breathe. My
heart and lungs were full of inflammation along with the rest of my
body. I didn't have the energy to put one foot in front of the other.

Thoughts raced through my mind. I wanted to scream but
could barely breathe a whisper. I just sat there lonely, afraid, shattered, broken, and completely empty inside.

Should I check myself into the hospital?

*What if they admit me in the psychiatric ward and won't let me go
home?*

Who will take care of Leah?

What if my friends find out?

Reaching for my phone, panic rushed over me like a tidal wave. A pool of tears cascaded down my face, as I cried, *Jesus, please help me!* At that moment, I heard God say to me, "You always struggle so hard to hold on, but trust me and let go. Let me handle this. It is time for you to leave with Leah."

Sitting in my car, unable to move, I continued to pray and ask God questions like *How did I get here? I'm a Christian for heaven's sake! Things like this just don't happen to Christian women—or do they?* I feel like such a failure.

Looking back now, I can see how years of worry and stress had brought me to that day—concerns about my family's future with drugs and alcohol abuse, stress from my adult boys making poor decisions, and my middle son in jail in another state, which all caused erratic panic attacks. Worry about Leah and the drugs, the meth, she found created knots in my stomach. Then, I had the stress of knowing, but not able to prove at the time, a drug dealer, a family member of Darren's living with us, who threatened to have me killed if I said anything to anyone about the meth. Struggling trying to keep my sanity resulted in midnight crying sessions, not to mention there I was trying to recuperate from a fall that I became paralyzed from where I had to have a four-level neck fusion surgery to keep me from dying, with absolutely no help from my husband who was consumed with his meth addiction.

My concerns consumed me. Worrying became my addiction, demanding my ongoing attention. I was trying to "hold it all together" on the outside, but on the inside, a sea of doubt and fear haunted me.

Maybe you're in a similar place. Have the stresses of life caught up with you too? Are you worried about your finances, health, marriage, job, or kids? Do you wonder if anyone sees your pain or even cares? If you're brave enough to cry out for help, will anyone rescue you?

In today's verse, we are reminded we do have a rescuer:

> The eyes of the *Lord* are on the righteous,
> and His ears are open to their cry for help …

the righteous cry out, and the *Lord* hears, and delivers them from all their troubles. The *Lord* is near the brokenhearted; He saves those crushed in spirit. (Psalm 34:15–18)

God sees you and hears your cries for help, even when no one else does. He knows your heartache. He sees your pain. If your heart is broken and you feel crushed from all sides, God promises to be close to you. Though you may not see him with your physical eyes, he is there.

God rescued me that day. After several hours of prayer, God calmed my heart, and I called my dad. I reached out to my family for help, and the healing started. I moved out with Leah with the support of my dad, sisters, and brother. I filed for divorce. Although I wanted an instant miracle, it took time, but God never left my side. As I prayed, God gave me the strength for the next step. He guided me along a journey that led to true freedom, for which I am forever grateful. I see so clearly now my prayers being answered over the next few years. God had to work on us all individually for my prayers to be answered.

Humble yourselves, therefore, under God's mighty hand, that he may lift you up in due time. (1 Peter 5:6)

We were set apart not set aside. We were set apart, given individual assignments that required preparation. God had a work to do in us *all*, in order for my prayers to be answered.

Chapter 18

Give Up or God Up

*Therefore, since God in his mercy has given
us this new way, we never give up.*

2 Corinthians 4:1

REPLACE THE HOPELESSNESS WITH HAPPINESS with God.

Problems kept piling up—many of which I had no power or resources to resolve. I was living in survival mode and found myself simply spent.

One morning, after another set of seemingly hopeless issues reared their ugly heads, tears began to roll. I let out a heavy sigh and in a quivering voice spoke out loud, "God, I literally don't think I can take anymore."

Maybe you can relate—your life feels out of control and change seems hopeless.

The day I called out to the Lord and said, "I can't take this anymore," I felt like giving up. Maybe you've felt that way too.

But upon uttering those words and admitting my weakness, I felt a nudge to my spirit. I knew I needed to focus on God instead of my circumstances and worries. I needed to refocus on what he had done in my life, rather than what he had not yet done. I needed to believe instead of doubt him and place my trust in the only One who actually could fix things.

As I intentionally adjusted my focus on God, hope and peace slowly returned. Faith alone helped me to God-up instead of give up, not because I had the strength to do so, but because I had God's strength within me that pushed me forward in faith, just like the Apostle Paul.

In 2 Corinthians 4, Paul encouraged the church at Corinth not to give up. He reminded the people they each held a treasure in their heart—the spirit of God—which was the sole reason they could persevere when they felt like quitting in the face of adversities, especially when it came to defending the Gospel.

2 Corinthians 4:1 says, "Therefore, since God in his mercy has given us this new way, we never give up." We see proof that although he stumbled, Paul consistently focused on God. The "new way" because we have his spirit within us since Jesus died on the cross. Instead, we can enjoy the gifts of grace, mercy, hope, and strength.

We read throughout scripture that every time Paul wanted to give up, he chose to God-up instead. He chose to depend on God's power and strength instead of his own.

Paul's faith equipped and inspired him to keep going to God, despite earthly, common-sense reasons to quit. Over his lifetime, Paul suffered greatly—he was imprisoned, beaten, stoned, shipwrecked, chased mercilessly by enemies, and lived fearfully in caves.

He suffered mental and spiritual exhaustion in addition to physical pain, hunger, thirst, and difficult living conditions. That's enough to make anyone want to give up! Yet despite his weakest moments, he never did.

The choices Paul made each day to God-up instead of give up filled him with strength and perseverance he could have never found on his own.

Maybe for reasons only you and God know, you've found yourself saying, "I can't take anymore," too. Maybe giving up hope about that difficult situation, problem, or relationship seems easier than hanging on to it. It's okay. Everyone struggles with those thoughts and feelings at times. But like Paul, the moment we catch ourselves feeling that way we can choose to give up or God-up.

We can let our thoughts and feelings deplete us of strength, hope, and joy; or we can lean fully into God and ask for him to carry us in our weakest moments.

When we God-up, instead of give up, God will always show up.

When I'm tired and I really do secretly want to give up, I need God to fill my heart with peace, to help me see him at work in the situations in my life and trust he is in control. I need God to replace my hopelessness with happiness.

Chapter 19

God Is There for Us All

Jesus said, "Apart from me you can do nothing."

THIS IS SO TRUE. GOD is not holding out on you. He actually likes it when we ask for his help.

When you are hurting, in trouble, or waiting for answers in your life, you need to believe that your help has been sent out from heaven and is on its way.

The Bible repeatedly tells us that God is our helper. So can we really trust God to help us? Yes, we really can!

It's so easy to agree with that right away, and there are a lot of things we mentally ascent to. But when it comes to practically applying them in our everyday life, we can't seem to find a way to do it.

I'll let you in on a secret—you need to ask God for help because the Holy Spirit is not the type to barge into your life and take over.

Have you ever had someone try to push their opinions or their agenda on you? That's not the way we work, and it certainly isn't the way the Holy Spirit does either.

The Holy Spirit knows the answer to every problem, and he will help you through each one. But he won't give you his advice unless you ask for it. In other words, humble up and ask God for the help.

Every problem matters to God.

"God is not holding out on you."

Jesus said, "Apart from me you can do nothing." And that's so true. God is not holding out on you; he actually likes it when we ask for his help.

Darren at this point was wanting help with his addiction. He started going to AA and praying for God to release him from his addition.

In Psalms, we frequently see King David going to God for help. "Be pleased to save me, Lord; come quickly, Lord, to help me" (Psalm 40:13). Notice that David was bold enough to ask God for help, but he was also confident that God would answer his prayers. We should all learn from that!

Darren went to a store with Leah while we were first separated and encountered what he calls an angel. This angel was an older gentleman with a walker. He needed help getting something from the top shelf on an isle that Darren and Leah were on. Leah asked if she could help him. The older gentleman sparked a conversation with Leah and asked her if she believed in Jesus and if she knew the Lord's Prayer. Leah said yes, and the gentleman asked her to recite the Lord's Prayer for him. She did. The old man turned to Darren and said, "I can see something is weighing heavy on your heart." Darren said, "Yes, I am an alcoholic and a meth addict. My wife and I are separated and going through a divorce." The old man told him, "No, you can't divorce your wife. You need Jesus." He also told Darren if he would turn his life over to Jesus Christ, follow Jesus, and not worry about his family, and they will follow.

We all have so many things in life that seem to bring us down, but God wants us to stay strong in him like David did. I think this old man or angel that Darren met that day in the store was sent by God with a message. Darren took this message seriously and began changing his life. He decided at that moment to give his life to the Lord.

He went to a church in Riverside, Texas, the next morning, which was Easter. He went to the altar, confessed his sins, and dedicated his life to the Lord that day.

Those who do will eventually come out on top, because there's no way the enemy can hold you back if you will trust God and keep your hope in him.

Learn how to trust your helper.

Not only will God deliver you, but also he will sustain you while you're waiting for your breakthrough. He keeps us strong while we're waiting and keeps us from going under.

Even when we are tempted to think, *It's not going to do me any good to pray after the things I have done, or the way I have acted,* we can't let that stop us for asking for God's help. Why is that? Because when we go to the Father in prayer, we don't go in our name. We go in the name of Jesus.

When you're hurting, in trouble, or waiting for answers in your life, you need to believe that your help has been sent out from heaven, and it is on the way. God may not come early, but he won't ever be late.

No matter what your circumstances look like or what the world may say, hang in there, because help is on the way!

Darren was now developing a relationship with the Lord. He consumed every day with something involving God. He started going to church with some really good friends of ours, Mark and Leigh. He went to a Bible study they held in their home on Sunday nights. He went to the Cowboy Church on Monday night and went to AA on Tuesday, Wednesday, and Thursday nights. He was emerging himself with God. He had battled addiction his whole life, and after the encounter with the old man in the store that today we feel like was an angel sent from God, Darren was trying a different approach of filling that hole that he was trying to fill with drugs and alcohol. He was filling that hole with Jesus.

Chapter 20

The Lord Says to Wait and Trust

*Many are the plans in a Man's heart, but it is
the purpose of the Lord that prevails.*
—Proverbs 19:21

DO YOU EVER FEEL AS though you want to take matters into your own hands, plot a course of action, and then set sail despite all warning signs that tell you to just wait? To wait on God is a hard one for me. I have always been an impatient, take charge, make-things-happen kind of girl. As Christ-followers, we know that God has a plan for our lives; but waiting to hear God's voice, waiting for his plan to unfold, becomes overwhelming; and we take over, charting our own journey, often with disastrous results. For me, taking matters into my own hands has never been a good idea.

As Darren and I proceeded with our divorce, we gathered our armies to take with us to court. I had my family and one close friend Linda who had been one of my best friends since high school. She is the only friend I had confided in, at this time, because of embarrassment and because she had recently divorced her husband who was also a meth addict. She knew firsthand what I was going through. Darren was out rallying his troops and in doing so was pointing fingers at everyone else but himself. He was spreading rumors about me and my oldest son DJ. These rumors were very heartbreaking, as people were calling me and telling me what he was saying. This was a side of Darren I had never seen. He was going through detox off the meth, and that was the only excuse I could see for this behavior. I was still seeing the counselor in Hockley at the church we had been attending for a few years. This counselor knew a lot about meth and meth addicts, as his sister was a meth addict, and he had custody of her children. He told me that what Darren was doing by pointing fingers at everyone else, but himself, was a classic action of an addict. They will point fingers at everyone else to take the spotlight off themselves. In doing this, Darren had most of our friends in Waller County convinced I was addicted to prescription drugs, which would be easy to believe, as I was seen out during the time I was over medicated.

I was still prescribed hydrocodone, which I took on occasion at night, for back and neck pain. The rest of the medication I had got off six months prior to leaving Darren and filing for divorce because I could not function while taking all that was prescribed to me. Most of these friends had not seen me in almost a year, as I was no longer going around anywhere where my family would be drinking. They had no idea what medication I was taking and what I wasn't. I was so done with alcohol and drugs that it would literally make me sick to be around my family when they were drinking. I had seen the damage it had done to my family, and I was done with it all. Months before I left Darren, I had quit going anywhere with him where I knew he would be drinking.

When we went to court, my sister testified that she knew Darren was using meth, and my friend Linda testified that Darren had told her he was using meth.

Darren had almost all our friends from Waller in court with him. He had two of them testify. They both said that they were aware of Darren's meth use, that they were aware of Darren's abuse of hydrocodone, and that they also knew that Darren was stealing my hydrocodone and that I would have to hide it from him. Then, when these same two friends were asked about me, they said that I was angry and crazy and that they would not allow their child to ever be with me. But that they would allow their child to be with Darren, a meth addict.

This was probably one of the most painful experiences in my life. I did not understand how my husband could convince so many people that I thought were my friends to turn against me, when he was an admitted alcoholic and meth addict that fought the addiction for most of his life.

But this is what divorce does. It causes people to choose sides without knowing the whole story. As I remember my father saying when his sister went through a divorce, "There's his story. There's her story, and God only knows the truth." There is so much truth in this statement. I will say that when I left Darren and took Leah and we went to my dad's home, I did not contact or tell anyone but my family and one friend. I did not want to tell our story to everyone, as I did not think it was my place to tell everyone about Darren's meth addiction. It was his story to tell. But I had no idea the extremes he would go in damaging me and my oldest son's reputation.

Because of going through detox, he had so much anger. He was blaming my oldest son for our divorce. I still don't understand that one at all, other than his brain was really messed up during that time, due to the detox of coming off meth. I had done some research on the subject and read that it takes a year for the brain to function normally if it ever does again, after coming off meth.

I wanted so desperately to tell the world what a liar Darren was. Sitting back and watching him destroy the reputation of my son and myself was so painful.

I actually tried to give this one to the Lord. I prayed that God would reveal the lies Darren was spreading about my son and me.

In this world of "go, see, do," and "make things happen," "waiting and trusting" is perhaps the hardest thing of all.

Seek his presence and dwell in it, wait on him, and trust him. Three simple phrases, three very difficult concepts to master for me.

So we fret, and we worry, and we calculate, and we seek advice from far too many people, and we talk when we should be silent, and we do everything we possibly can to keep ourselves busy, because *that's* what society tells us to do.

Oh, but how opposite are the plans of the Lord.

Seek his presence and dwell in it. Wait on him. Trust him.

What if in mastering these three concepts, we could each find that "purpose and why" that we all so desperately seek?

Proverbs 19:21 says, "Many are the plans in a Man's heart, but it is the purpose of the Lord that prevails."

If we can wait and not manipulate, God promises us he is always at work for our good (Romans 8:28). Even when the situation seems to be going the wrong way, we can trust that his way is best. We must be prayerful, wait, and trust. Easier said than done, though, I know.

Yet when we wait and see God's goodness come to pass, we create a history with God, a collection of faith moments when we have seen God's faithfulness. This foundation builds our faith in him so we know we can trust him again and again.

I knew all these things, but I wanted so desperately for the truth to be revealed.

Chapter 21

Let's Find the Gold in Everyone

Anyone can find the dirt in someone.
Be the one that finds the gold.

—Proverbs 11:27

I WAS LOOKING FOR SOMETHING to watch on TV one night and turned on *Girl Meets World*. I found myself so intrigued as I watched the episode "Girl Meets Flaws." This episode quickly became one I could relate to on so many levels. It had quite a few lessons for just half an hour. Riley was worried about what her friends think of her. Billy was jealous of his friends that led him to be mean in order to make himself feel better. Farkle was told he was nothing, so he believed it.

I always thought I was a confident person, until going through my separation and divorce in the courts, which got *very* ugly, very fast, and left scars that are slowly healing, three years later. I've heard that you spend your whole life getting over things that happen in your past. The more I think about that, the truer it becomes. Going through that time in my life was literally a living *hell*. I'm not cussing here but talking about what I think of as *hell*.

The first lesson Mr. Matthews in *Girl Meets World* was teaching the class is that "sometimes the world presents you with opportunities to show who you really are. Will you have the courage to stand up to someone who tries to take your spirit away?"

The second lesson was how to respond when people are mean. Lucas said, "Don't let what anybody says about you, get to you; that's what gives them power." Boy, could I relate to that one. During our divorce, there were so many lies, rumors, and fabricated stories running through the rumor mill of our small town. I just wanted to run and hide from the embarrassment, even though in my heart I knew most of what was being said and spread were lies. The truth has a way of always coming out. It may take a few days or years, but the truth is usually revealed.

I have found in the past few years of doing lots of Bible studies that as you get closer to God, a true relationship with him, you won't care what anyone says or thinks. The only one that truly matters is God, and he already knows the truth.

What a freedom!

Another lesson was that people change. I love that when Billy was being mean, they still worried for their friend. Riley was wondering why Billy didn't see that he did anything wrong. Maya turns to Riley, like she always does, and says, "Riley, you can't fix everything. Okay, go ahead." (I absolutely love that and relate to Riley because I totally try to fix everything too.) At the end of the episode, the kids in the class owned up to their flaws and wrote them on their foreheads. They did this as a way to show Billy it was okay to have flaws.

When asked about their foreheads, Maya said, "When I own it, it doesn't make me feel so bad."

Then, Mr. Matthews handed them wipes and said, "We're all human beings. We're all on the same team and if we sense our own flaws because we see them in others; it's a true friend who help us wipe them away."

A friend of mine posted on Facebook this quote, "Anyone can find the dirt in someone. Be the one that finds the gold" (Proverbs 11:27). So, I looked up the verse that says, "If you search for good, you will find favor; but if you search for evil, it will find you!" I want to live like that. I want to see the best in people always. I want to be the one who finds the gold in everyone and everything around her. I want to search for the good.

Growing up, I heard my mother say at least a hundred times, "If you don't have something nice to say about someone, don't say anything at all." I fell into the trap of gossip just like everyone else. I usually hear my mother's voice saying, "If you don't have something nice to say about someone, don't say anything at all." As soon as I open my mouth, I feel the guilt, and I try to find something good to say about the person being talked about. I'm not always successful, but I'm working hard on it.

It's been said that knowledge is power. Unfortunately, many people like to spread damaging information or intimate details about others, whether true or not. This is what is called gossip. People used to call gossip as dishing the dirt. Whatever it's called, people use gossip to hurt people, in order to feel good about themselves and to feel like they have power over others.

When Darren and I were going through our divorce, in the court, there were so many lies and rumors going around. They were spreading faster than a forest fire in a drought, and there was not enough water on earth to put them out and stop the spread. I know because I was frantically trying to put them out. This was *not* a smart idea on my part. When I try to handle things by myself, my way, it always gets me in trouble. I should have let God handle the rumors and the people spreading them. He can handle anything we give him a whole lot better than we can. These rumors were so damaging to so many lives. And most of the rumors were absolutely *not* true.

The most dangerous part about gossip is that it steals another person's reputation. A reputation is very fragile. When you gossip, you are helping to destroy something extremely valuable. With gossip, there is no way of knowing what is truth or lies.

There's an old saying, "stick and stones can break my bones, but words will never hurt me," that's just not true. I don't care how old you are. Being gossiped about can be extremely painful. If you don't want it done to you, don't do it to others. In the end, it never pays to gossip.

"What does the Bible say about spreading rumors and gossip?"

A rumor is an unconfirmed, widely spread story or statement. Rumors may or may not contain elements of truth, but their validity is anyone's guess—rumors carry no factual certainty. Rumors are also known as gossip, and the Bible has a lot to say about that.

Scripture warns against spreading rumors and those who engage in gossip. Proverbs 20:19 says, "A gossip betrays a confidence; so avoid anyone who talks too much." Words are powerful. They can build up or destroy (Proverbs 18:21). James 3:2–12 instructs us to control our words, stating in verse 5, "Consider a great forest is set on fire by a small spark." Spreading "harmless" rumors, then, can cause great destruction. God desires that we use our words to praise him (Psalm 34:1), to speak wisdom (Proverbs 10:13), and to encourage and edify each other (1 Thessalonians 5:11; Ephesians 4:29).

The Bible often includes gossip in lists of specific evils (2 Corinthians 12:20; Romans 1:29). Spreading rumors is so repulsive in the Lord's sight that he made a prohibition against it in the Law he gave to the Israelites (Leviticus 19:16). 1 Timothy 5:13 sternly warns against using idle time to spread slander. And Proverbs 17:4 implies that those who eagerly listen to gossip have low character.

So why do we enjoy the rumor mill? Proverbs 26:22 gives one reason, "The words of a gossip are like choice morsels; they go down to the inmost parts." There is a delicious thrill in hearing scandalous information about someone we know or wish we knew. Jealousy is often the root of spreading rumors. When we learn "the real reason" someone did something, we can alter our opinion of him or her and make ourselves feel better by comparison. We rarely hear rumors that exalt someone's reputation. We don't hear rumors that someone's son worked hard to make the honor roll again, that a friend's spouse is kind and devoted, or that the Joneses saved for ten years to take that luxury cruise. That kind of information is not a "choice morsel." Instead, we perk up when we hear that someone's son cheated his way onto the honor roll, that a friend's spouse only pretends to be kind and devoted because he is having an affair, or that the Joneses blew their retirement to take that luxury cruise. Those kinds of tid-bits let us compare ourselves favorably with the ones gossiped about, and we feel more satisfied with our own lives.

Proverbs 26:20 gives us the antidote for spreading rumors, "Without wood a fire goes out; without a gossip a quarrel dies down."

We cannot stop all rumors, but we can refuse to participate in them. We can break the "telephone" chain and refuse to pass it on. When we hear slanderous news, we should go to the source and check it out. If we are not part of the solution, and the person we are telling is not part of the solution, then the news is not ours to propagate. Our sinful natures enjoy possessing a juicy morsel of information that would gain us attention in the telling. But when we are willing to recognize the selfishness of that desire, we can repent of it and dedicate our mouths to the glory of God (Psalm 19:14).

On the last day Darren and I went to court, the judge ordered him to leave the house. I got everything I wanted. I got custody of Leah, I got the house, I got the child support amount I wanted, and I got the alimony amount I wanted. Darren had to continue paying me and Leah's insurance and cell phone bill. The only thing I had to pay was the utility bill. In my eyes, I had won. But had I really won?

The weekend I moved back into the house, Darren had Leah for the weekend. My family had come to help me clean, do the yard, and clean out the barn, which was an absolute disaster. As we worked our way through the barn, I saw a sheet in the back corner covering something. As I pulled the sheet off the stuff, my heart hit the floor. It was everything that Darren had told everyone that DJ had stolen and sold. I was livid. I took pictures of all the stuff and started sending pictures of what I found in the barn to everyone he had told that DJ had stolen the stuff. I felt like it was my job to clear DJ's name and reveal the lie that Darren had told about him.

After sending this picture out, I had one of the friends who testified against me in court and said that I was angry and crazy. She texted me back and told me to quit enabling my children. Well, that just didn't sit too well with me, especially when I knew some stuff about her husband and never said a word to her or anyone else. So, in the heat of the moment, I told her to stay out of my business and to mind her own business, and she might want to start with her own husband. I was just sending them the picture to clear my son's name as I knew the lies Darren had told them.

This was probably the biggest mistake I have ever made in my life. You should never take matters in your own hands. I should have given the matter to God and let him fight this battle for me. Being angry just opened the door to Satan. The next thing I knew, this woman's husband was flying down our street. He was going so fast he went airborne over the hill coming down our road. He flew up the driveway where me and my family were standing in the porte-cochère, and he got out of his truck. I could tell by looking at him he was so drunk. He had such a fire in his eyes. He pulled a rifle out, cocked it, pointed it at us, and said, "Tessie, I have a gift for you. I'm going to take you out." My sister started screaming, "Are you crazy? There are kids here." He snapped and got into his truck and pulled out as fast as he came in.

The next few months, I lived in constant fear. I had Darren's family member threaten to have me killed if I told anyone about the meth. Now, I had someone come to my home with a gun threatening me. There was not a doubt in my mind that if I would have been home alone that night, he would have shot me. If he had the guts to pull the gun out and cock it in front of a group of people, there is not a doubt in my mind that if I would have been home alone, he would have pulled the trigger.

I know God was with me that day and protected me.

Chapter 22

God's Call to be Set Apart

Know that the Lord has set apart his faithful servant
for himself; the Lord hears when I call to him.

—Psalm 4:3

"There is something wonderfully sacred that happens when a girl chooses to look past being set aside to see God's call for her to be set apart."

This is one of my favorite quotes by Lysa Terkeurst from her Bible study, "Uninvited."

Have you ever felt like you have been set aside?

Rejection is the most common emotional wound we sustain in daily life. Our risk of rejection used to be limited by the size of our immediate social circle. Today, thanks to electronic communications, social media, and dating apps, each of us is connected to thousands of people, any of whom might ignore us and leave us feeling rejected as a result.

In addition to these kinds of minor rejections, we are still vulnerable to serious and more devastating rejections as well. When our spouse leaves us, get fired from our jobs, betrayed by our friends, or ostracized by our families and communities for our choices, the pain we feel can be absolutely devastating.

> Turn to me and be gracious to me, for I am
> lonely and afflicted. The troubles of my heart
> are enlarged; bring me out of my distresses.
> (Psalm 25:16–17)

Have you ever felt set aside? I sure have. After doing the Bible study "Uninvited," my eyes were open to why I was set aside or set apart. God wanted me to himself so he could talk to me alone and without any outside influences.

Throughout scripture, God sets apart his people for himself and his purposes. Set aside for a divine purpose, boy does that put things in perspective.

Often, the Bible uses the language of holiness to describe this act of setting apart. In Psalm 4:3, however, the language is slightly different though the idea is the same. Here, God distinguishes those who are godly, because they have received God's faithful love. In other words, Psalm 4:3 does not mean if we make ourselves godly, then God will set us apart. Rather, God sets us apart in his mercy, making a covenant with us based on his salvation. He makes us godly so that we might live in a godly manner. Living in a godly manner is living by God's Words, following his commands in the Bible. If you ever have a decision to make, I guarantee you can find the right decision if you set yourself apart from the world and their views. Open the Bible and begin reading, praying, and listen for God's command through the Holy Spirit. Sometimes, you need to be set apart, alone with God, really alone with God to pray, without any outside influences.

Even Jesus was set apart when he went to the Garden of Gethsemane to pray.

After he heard about his friend, John the Baptist, he withdrew to a deserted place by himself. After he fed the five thousand, where there was a rush of ministry success, we are told he "went up the mountain by himself to pray."

Luke speaks about this in a way that implies there's a regular practice going on here:

> Jesus would withdraw to deserted places
> and pray. (Luke 5:16)

He teaches his disciples to do the same thing. This is solitude.

In solitude, I withdraw from people, noise, cell phones, computers, television, and all the stimulation of life to be with God. I myself get away from all of the scaffolding in my life, all of my roles, and all of the people who are either cheering me on or telling me I ought to do something different. I get away from all of that to just be alone with God "to find out," *Is there anything really just between God and me?* Absolutely!

I realize I have a *life*. It's way bigger than what I do. It's way bigger than what anybody thinks of me. I have this *life* that without God as my influence, it just does not work!

The emphasis in Psalm 4:3 is not about how we live in our godliness. Rather, this verse underscores the fact that the Lord has set us apart "for himself." We belong to him, not primarily to do his work, but because he loves us and seeks a relationship with us.

Here is today's good news: God has set you apart for himself. God wants a relationship with you and to be able to talk to you alone. He seeks intimacy with you so that you might know his amazing love.

Here are two thoughts that might encourage you today?

1. Look for the gift of being humbled.

Proverbs 11:2 reminds us that "with humility comes wisdom." In this set-apart place, God will give you much-needed special wisdom for the assignment ahead, which is his plan for you.

2. Look for the gift of silence.

Had I been surrounded by the voices around me, I would have surely missed the voice of God. I'm trying to bring more silence into my day now so I can whisper, "God, what might you want to say to me right now? I'm listening."

I know it can be painful to be alone. And I know the thoughts of being set aside are loud and overwhelmingly tempting to believe in the feeling unnoticed and uninvited.

But as you pray through your feelings, ask God if your situation has more to do with you being prepared than overlooked.

"There is something wonderfully sacred that happens when a girl chooses to look past being set aside to see God's call for her to be set apart."

I'm believing today that I'm set apart, not set aside.

After Leah and I got settled back into our home, I looked around, and it looked like the aftermath of a war zone. Everything was dead. I had gotten everything I wanted out of the divorce, but I was still not happy. My life seemed awful. I was so depressed. I didn't have the energy to do much of anything than try to survive. I had withdrawn from everyone, even my family. Looking back, I was set apart from the world, set apart for God and God alone. God needed to work on me and continue with his assignment, his plan for my life. I needed to be able to hear his voice without any outside influences.

My health continued to deteriorate at a rapid pace. I was living on steroid shots and prednisone for the many autoimmune diseases I had developed. I was also put on methotrexate, a low-dose chemo, trying to boost my immune system to kick in and start working again. Nothing was working.

I started praying like I had never prayed before. I had been doing a divorce recovery class for about three months in Katy. We were getting to the end of our book, the final chapter. It was what divorce should look like. There were three places you could go, divorced and remain friends. Well, I knew there was no way that was going to happen. You could divorce and hate each other and never be able to be in the same room together. Now, that I could see happening at this point. Or you could reconcile, which was what God ultimately wanted. The couple leading my group were married to each other, but it wasn't their first marriages. They both shared with our group that if they had to do it over again, they would have fought harder to make their marriages work that they had kids with. Yes, I heard what they said, but thought no way in this lifetime was that going to happen. Darren was also doing a divorce recovery class at a different church, which neither of us knew the other was doing the class. I found out later he was doing the same chapter about the same time I was and was having the same thoughts I was. At this point, we literally hated each other and could not be in the same room together and be civil.

I continued to pray for God to show me happiness again.

Leah had her friend Gracie spend the night. We were up getting ready to go to church. Leah and I were still attending the church in Hockley that we had attended as a family prior to our separation. Leah and I were still getting counseling there as well.

Gracie's parents came to pick her up to go to their church, and Leah said that she wanted to go with Gracie to her church. I said, "That's fine." I don't care where we go to church as long as we went to church somewhere.

We walked into Lifehouse Bible Church and sat down. The couple in front of me turned and introduced themselves to us.

The gentleman said, "Hi. I'm Lonnie McCaffety, and this is my wife Pat.

I said, "Is Betty, your sister?"

He said, "Yes."

I told him I was Tessie Fraysur and my dad was Rudy Zajac, who was dating his sister. They had been dating for several years. Everyone in that church was so warm and friendly and made us feel so welcome.

Pastor Randy's message that day was directed right at me. It was all about forgiveness, Matthew 6:14 to be exact.

> For if you forgive other people when they sin against you, your heavenly Father will also forgive you. But if you don't forgive others for their sins, your father will not forgive your sins.

Wow, this was an eye-opener for me. I was a sinner needing forgiveness from God. Being raised Catholic, this was serious business for me. I lived most of my early years in elementary school, junior high, and high school going to confession quite often. It was the way I was raised. I made the Sacrament of Reconciliation in second grade. So, I knew all about the importance of forgiveness of sin.

So my new prayer was for God to help me forgive Darren. I really liked this new church and the pastor and his wife Nikki, who both knew the Bible, and they knew it well. I liked the fact that it was a Bible-based church, with some great teaching that was right out of the Bible. This church was a lot smaller than the church we had been attending, so Leah and I continued to go for the next few weeks. The message of the sermon the next few weeks was still about forgiveness and directed right to me.

A sweet lady at the church, Regina, asked me to join their Bible study every Thursday morning. I thought, *That's exactly what I needed*. I had done Bible studies years ago, in my late twenties and early thirties and really enjoyed that time in my life. Looking back, it was the most peaceful time in my life. But now, fourteen years since I had done any type of Bible study, I had pretty much for-gotten anything I had learned. I went to the first Bible study, and it was the study called Stuck. Then, we did the study Storm Inside. Both of these Bible studies were exactly what I needed for this time in my life. I was stuck with a storm inside! These studies helped me hear even more from the Holy Spirit. I really enjoyed these new Christian friends I had in my life, and they truly cared about each other. I missed having true Christian friends who knew God's Word and were living and applying his Word to their lives.

As Thanksgiving started approaching, I found myself getting more depressed. At this point, I feel like I was hitting rock-bottom. I had never been this depressed before in my life. I was crying all the time, which is not like me.

After Thanksgiving dinner, Darren came to get Leah for the weekend. After he left with her, I lost it. This was the day I hit my rock-bottom. I laid face down on the cold tile floor in the game room and sobbed for hours, crying out to God, to please deliver me from this darkness, heal me, and comfort me. I pleaded with God telling him that I would do whatever he asked me to do. Anything, I would do it. I needed to be delivered out of this deep dark pit I was in. I asked him to grab my hand, to pull me out. At that moment I heard him say loud and clear, "Go work on your marriage." I thought, *Okay, is this God or Satan talking to me?* I was thoroughly confused. I said, "But God, you told me to leave and to file for divorce." I ended up falling asleep on the cold tile floor of the game room.

That night, I had one of the first dreams I remembered in years. I dreamed about me and Darren when we first got married, before the alcohol and drugs, before all the craziness, and before all the hate. In this dream, we were in love, and everything was beautiful. We were walking in fields of beautiful colorful flowers; then, we would be on the boat at a lake, just the two of us, watching a gorgeous sunset. I woke up sobbing once again, as I missed that life. I asked God, "What happened? Where did that life go? Where did those two people who were so much in love go?"

Once again, I heard the voice of God, and he said, "That was the life you had before Satan came in and destroyed everything."

Still not sure I was hearing from God or still dreaming, I continued to pray.

One of my favorite sayings used to be, "I know God promises to never give me more than I can handle, but sometimes, I think he must think I'm Superwoman." I'm sure most of you have heard me say that a time or two!

When trials come and life seems hard, we plead with God to deliver us from the problem when many times, his plan is to deliver us in the problem.

Praise does not depend on an understanding of the circumstance or trial. Praise depends on an understanding of who God really is and wants to be in our life and on our willingness to put our faith in him.

As humans, we will never fully understand God—this side of heaven. God is holy and without blemish. God is all-powerful and omniscient. He is the Creator of the universe and lives in you and me at our invitation. He is the only true, living God!

We may understand some of his ways and grasp the reasoning behind some of his plans. We may even come to the place of knowing him on what I call an intimate level, but a full understanding of God is reserved for heaven. Until then, we walk by faith, not by sight. I have learned to praise him in the darkness, knowing that the light is just ahead. I trust him for things I cannot see.

Most people who know me well would describe me as a strong person, someone who can usually handle what life throws at me. I thought the same thing until I became a powerless prisoner in the pit of darkness, as Satan took over my world. It took me a long time to climb out of that dark pit, but in the process, I learned many important truths.

I learned that I couldn't depend on my own strength or my fickle emotions. God often asked me to praise him when there didn't seem to be a whole lot to praise him for. I didn't feel like praising him.

I began to understand that praise is not a feeling.

Praise is a choice, a step of obedience taken without the assurance of a changed circumstance or the elimination of a trial.

Praise focuses on God, not the circumstance, and fixes its gaze on God's truth and God's character instead of on the trial at hand.

We can celebrate the battle before it even begins because the outcome is neither our responsibility nor our goal.

Praise begins and ends with faith in the very nature, personality, and integrity of God, and that never changes.

No matter what lies ahead, God is faithful.

No matter how hot the fiery trial might be, God is with us and will deliver us in it or from it.

So praise God!

Chapter 23

When God's Plan Is Preparing
You for Tomorrow's Surprise

*Feor I know the plans I have for you, says the Lord. They are plans
for good and not for evil, to give you a future and a hope."*
—Jeremiah 29:11

GOD'S PLAN WON'T ALWAYS BE what you think the final outcome is.
Sometimes, his ways surprise us.

When I think about the day I walked out on Darren and my
marriage, I find myself thinking about times when following God's
plan doesn't unfold as I thought it would.

The day I left, I would have bet a million dollars we would
have never reconciled. I'm not a gambler. As matter of fact, I hate
gambling because I hate losing money, even $10. But this is a bet I
would have made because I was so certain that I didn't see any way I
would ever consider going back, so that would have been a sure win
of a million dollars for me.

When I'm praying for open doors, they remain closed; when
I'm pleading for a answers, the answer don't seem to come; when I'm
asking for change, everything seems to stay the same. I remind myself
of the truth that I once learned—a frustrating time may be setting
the stage for a forthcoming victory.

After all, we have a loving Father who knows things we don't.
And sometimes, he needs to "wreck" our agenda in order to render his.

Jeremiah 29:11 reminds us that, ultimately, God's plans for us are good, "For I know the plans I have for you, says the Lord. They are plans for good and not for evil, to give you a future and a hope."

It takes faith to believe that promise when life isn't going as we'd expected. But I'm learning that we don't need to understand all of God's ways to accept his will. We simply need to trust his heart. The Bible reminds us God is love (1 John 4:8), and God is kind (Psalm 116:5). God is for us, not against us (Romans 8:31). We just need to make that first step when he tells us and listen for the next.

Sometimes, the step we hear him tell us to take makes no sense at all. But we need to be obedient to his command. When we remember who God is, we can more readily embrace what he's doing, even when we don't understand.

God's plans won't always mirror ours. And sometimes his ways surprise us. But I believe that, someday, when we look back at our lives through eternity's lens, we'll want to throw our arms around our faithful Father and say, "Thanks for spoiling my plans. Yours were even better!"

I know now that I had to obey God's command to go to Darren and tell him I wanted to try to reconcile our marriage, even after I know God told me to leave and file for a divorce.

I see God's plan of setting us apart so he could work on us individually. Darren found our Lord and savior after I left, and he got sober. This time, he wanted to get sober for himself and no one else. I needed that time away to also build a stronger relationship with our Lord, a time to become fully dependent on God for everything. I had to get to my rock-bottom to also turn to God to help me out of the deep dark pit of depression I found myself in. We needed time away from each other and time to spend with God to mend our broken hearts.

Chapter 24

If It's God's Plan, I Can Rest in It

Therefore, in the present case I advise you: Leave these men alone!
Let them go! For if their purpose or activity is of human origin,
it will fail. But if it is from God, you will not be able to stop
these men; you will only find yourselves fighting against God.
—Acts 5:38–39

THERE ARE TIMES I FELT God in every detail from the beginning to the end of something he called me to do. It was hard work, but I was grateful to do it, because God was directing my every step. I did everything I was supposed to do, and it turned out exactly the way I hoped.

This was one of those times I could hear God telling me to go work on my marriage, but I was just not feeling it. I knew that I needed to be obedient to God's command, and I did tell God I would do whatever he told me to do. I was so desperate that I decided, *What do I have to lose?* Darren is working a program, going to AA and to church or a bible study whenever he wasn't at an AA meeting. Maybe he was changing. People can change. I was seriously thinking about what God asked me to do. I was also finding myself forgiving him for the awful things that had happened at the end of our marriage. And when you start forgiving, you are left with love. I could feel a spark of the love starting to light in my heart. I was still very confused and did not understand why God would tell me to work on my marriage, now of all times.

I knew from my Christian upbringing that God expects obedience from me, and he expects me to obey whether others understand or not. His ways of doing things are sometimes much different than the way man thinks they should be done. He can see the big picture and has an awesome plan for us all. The only problem is that many times since we can't see things through God's eyes, we think that what he tells us to do doesn't make much sense. God always has everything under control, but many times, it sure doesn't look that way from where we are standing.

There are many instances in the Bible where God told people to do things that made absolutely no sense to them at the time, but when they obeyed, they saw the wondrous glory of God given to them and victory before their eyes.

I decided to move in obedience, still not 100 percent about this. I just knew that I heard what God told me to do, and I knew I needed to do it.

After a couple weeks of prayer, I decided to talk to Darren about what God told me to do. He was actually having the same feelings. So we decided to try to work on our marriage.

In reconciling, we felt we were doing everything Jesus had called us to do. It's was a mix of messy and beautiful, and we were okay with that. It wasn't easy, but it was worth it. I love the times I sense God doing something powerful and what God has called me to do.

I heard God's voice loud and clear during a time I was "set apart" from the world, and I was totally in tune to him alone. I listened to what God had to say to me, and he said loud and clear, "Go work on your marriage." I was a little confused at that moment, as God also told me nine months earlier to leave my husband and file for divorce. It is now that I look back on that time in my life that I understand God's plan. Darren and I had to go through that awful time in our life of separation and almost divorced to bring us to the beautiful place we are today. It was ugly, it was hard, and it was a lot of work. But I know without a doubt that God took us through that dark valley to bring us out totally dependent on him and his plan for our lives.

After reading in Acts, I know without a doubt that our reconciliation was God's plan. It gives me comfort in knowing that when it is God's plan and timing, I won't be stopped.

In today's passage, we find Peter and the apostles in a hard place. Despite their faithfulness, they have been jailed and beaten many times. They are human, so there are discouraging moments. Yet each time they are released, they go right back out and do what Jesus asked them to do.

At one point, their persistence troubles the authorities. They met to discuss their fate. That's when Gamaliel, a respected member of the community, speaks up,

> Let them go! For if their purpose or activity is of human origin, it will fail. But if it is from God, you will not be able to stop these men; you will only find yourselves fighting against God. (Acts 5:38–39)

If it is from God, you will not be able to stop them.

If we know God has asked us to do something, that's sufficient. All he wants is for us to do our part. We can trust he's doing his. We might not see the eternal impact, but he does.

There will always be a mix of messy (our feelings, critical people, and a desire to see immediate results) and faith as we follow Jesus. We might think it should be easier. We may believe it should bring us joy all the time. We might even equate off-the-charts results with pleasing him. On days like that, we need to remember this—if it is from God, you will not be able to stop. Nothing will stand in your way, not because of us, but because of him.

We can rest in what God's asked us to do, from beginning to end. We'll do our best. We'll be faithful. When we complete that assignment, we'll start listening for the next step. We keep our heart in tune to his voice.

If God is in it, and we know that to be true, we are free to simply show up and do our part. After all, God is in charge of the results.

Chapter 25

Reconciliation after Separation
Set Apart by God, for God

You can be sure of this: The Lord set apart the godly for himself. The Lord will answer when I call to him.

—Psalm 4:3

THROUGHOUT THE SCRIPTURE, GOD SETS apart people for himself and his purposes. Often, the Bible uses the language of holiness to depict this act of setting apart. In Psalm 4:3, however, the language is slightly different though the idea is the same. Here, God distinguishes those who are godly because they have received God's faithful love. In other words, Psalm 4:3 does not mean if we make ourselves godly, then God will set us apart. Rather, God sets us apart in his mercy, making a covenant with us based on his salvation. He makes us godly so that we live in our godliness. Rather, this verse underscores the fact that the Lord has set us apart "for himself." We belong to him, not primarily to do his work, but because he loves us and seeks relationship with us. We serve the Lord, therefore, in response to his invitation and in an intimate relationship with him.

Here is today's good news: God has set you apart for himself. God wants relationship with you. He seeks intimacy with you so that you might know his amazing love, and his plan for your life.

Once again, I found myself set apart. Darren and I together were set apart from everyone we knew, family and all our friends, as we tried working on our marriage. After you have shared all the dirt with your friends and family about each other, ultimately making them choose between the two of you, it makes it extremely hard for everyone to be happy for you when you decide to reconcile. It wasn't easy forgetting the betrayal of friends in a court room. My father was *not* happy at all. Can you blame him? He had cashed in many IRAs to help me pay my attorney and to support Leah and me for several months before the judge made her decision on what Darren was going to have to pay me. None of our family and friends understood what we were doing at all. My friends wanted nothing to do with Darren, and Darren's friends wanted nothing to do with me. So we were left *alone*, set apart, with no friends and no family. We were left alone with God. He wanted us all to himself so he could now work on us together. There is not a doubt in my mind that this is exactly how God wanted it. If we would have had any of those outside voices, giving us their opinions, a reconciliation would have never worked. We were both so broken inside. We needed God and each other to heal.

I know that God set us apart on the basis of *his* sovereign grace, not because of anything we had done. In no way are we godly enough to earn his favor. We were glad recipients of his grace, which binds us to him and helps us to be more like him.

He set us apart for himself, not just for him to work on us and our marriage, but first and foremost for a relationship with him. What an incredible privilege it is to know him, to have freedom to speak to him, to rely upon him, and to call him Father.

After Darren moved back into the house, Leah and I asked him if he would like to visit Lifehouse Bible Church with us. I shared with Darren how much Leah and I loved this church, the pastor, his wife, and the people in it. Darren agreed to go with us to this new church. When we went that first Sunday, once again the pastor's message in the sermon was directed right to us, and this went on for several months as we went back to this church. Darren felt the same way as Leah and I did about this new church, and we decided to make this our home church and become members. We really liked how small this church was and how everyone knew each other and genuinely cared about each other. We felt like that's where we belonged as a family.

Darren and I also got several weeks of marriage counseling from our pastor and his wife. The counseling we got from them was Bible-based, just like all the sermons on Sunday mornings. Our pastor and his wife shared with us what the Bible said about marriage, the role of the husband, and the role of the wife in the family. The most important thing we learned from them was that God needed to be in the center of our marriage. This truly changed our family dynamic. It was a way of living that we had never tried before, and it is working. It was hard to make the changes in our life, but change is never easy.

Chapter 26

A Hunger for God's Word

*He who began a good work in you will carry it on
to completion until the day of Christ Jesus.*
—Philippians 1:6

LONG BEFORE I KNEW GOD, he knew me and loved *me*.

I heard the whisper of God at a very young age. Having grandparents and parents who were devout in their faith truly influenced my belief in God.

Through the years, I lost that relationship with him through loss and grief. My trust in God became questionable.

For fourteen years, I was looking everywhere to fill that hole I was missing.

I craved something more than fun and diversion, more than a life of partying. But what? Looking back, I see my inner hunger drove me to search for ways to find myself again, but none of them worked.

My soul hungered for something more.

I saw my family falling apart long before I made some changes in me. I would pray for happiness and changes. It wasn't till I hit my rock-bottom that I turned back to God in desperation that I saw answered prayer.

Daily, I began to keep a journal, pray, and read Bible verses—something I used to do fourteen years ago when my life was at the best it had ever been prior to this time in my life. As I did, I felt a deep awakening in my heart, and power was flowing into me.

As I started to panic about my family and our crazy life, my first instinct kicked in. Suddenly, I stopped and prayed, for my family, for the craziness to end, for peace, for us all. It took three long years for this prayer to be answered.

Whoa. There really was something to this spiritual stuff. Through prayer and Bible reading, I began to understand why my heart felt so empty for the first time. I was hungry to be filled by God.

After I started going to Lifehouse Bible Church and listening to so many sermons that were directed right to me and everything I needed to hear for such a long time, I found a peace like I hadn't known in years. I had done several years of Bible studies in the past, but by this time in my life, I had forgotten anything and everything I had ever learned. The people at this new church knew a lot about God and the Bible. They were kind and welcoming. I knew we would be back after the first visit.

When I did a Bible study with the ladies at this church, we sat in a circle, prayed for each other, studied God's Word, and cried with each other. Their prayers made me feel cared for and encouraged, as if I mattered personally to them and to God. In doing the Bible studies, I started to read my Bible every day. I at one point was doing three Bible studies at one time. I was that hungry for God's Word.

In doing Bible studies and reading the Bible, I was hearing whispers of God daily. God was accomplishing his purposes in me and whispering his love through two powerful means—his Word and his people. God had begun "a good work" in me, and I knew he would "carry" it on to completion until the "day of Christ Jesus" (Philippians 1:6).

Today, I treasure those memories with these new Christian women God put in my life, at the perfect time. I consider this as a major milestone in my faith journey. Far before I knew God, he knew me and loved me. He never left my side, even when I turned away from him. He placed his Word in my life at a new church and sent me to the dear ladies at this church to sow seeds of faith into my life—seeds that have grown into a vibrant personal friendship with God and that continue to grow ever-deeper roots every day. The more I studied God's Word, the more my hunger began to grow, the hunger to know more of God's Word. Until you have to truly depend on God, you don't truly understand the power of God's Word. Studying God's Word has become a necessary part of my daily life.

Chapter 27

God Is in the Restoration Business

The Lord says, "I will give you back what you lost to the swarming locusts, the hopping locusts, the stripping locusts, and the cutting locust."
—Joel 2:24

The Lord will guide you always; he will satisfy your needs in a sun-scorched land and will strengthen your frame. You will be like a well-watered garden, like a spring whose waters never fail. Your people will rebuild the ancient ruins and will raise up the age-old foundations; you will be called Repairer of Broken Walls, Restorer of Streets with Dwellings.
—Isaiah 58:11–12

DURING OUR TIME OF RESTORING our marriage, we had some other great Christian friends who helped us through. Mark and Leigh Evans were two of the godly Christians who helped Darren with his walk with the Lord, after he had the encounter with the angel on Easter in 2014. While Darren and I were separated, Darren and Leah, when he had Leah on the weekend, would go with them to their church on Sunday mornings and then do a Bible study with them at their home on Sunday evenings.

After Darren and I started to try to work on our marriage, Leigh would call and check on us, giving us godly wisdom. She would invite us to Christian conferences, and we went to many over the next couple of years. I will never forget when we first started going to these different conferences, we kept hearing the same message over and over, of God restoring everything that Satan had stolen from us. This message was delivered by most of the pastors at the conferences we went to for several months.

The Holy Spirit was letting us know that God was going to restore everything that Satan had stolen from us, and he had taken almost everything we had. All we needed to do was expect it and rest in God's Word—REST, *R*estoration of *E*verything *S*atan *T*ook.

I first heard about this restoration of marriages, families, finances, etc., from Joseph Prince on a Christian television program I was watching while Darren and I were separated the week I moved back into the house. I never even entertained the thought that he might be talking to me. To tell you the truth, I don't even think I was grasping what he was saying until I heard it again through another pastor after Darren and I reconciled and were going to these conferences talking about restoration. I came home and found Joseph Prince's program online so I could listen to it again. I was starting to think, *Maybe the message was for me.*

In Joseph Prince's sermon, he proclaimed us to expect to receive God's much-more restoration. The wasted years, broken dreams, wrecked relationships—whatever your loss may be, look to the Lord for your much-more restoration! Everything he said lined up with scripture, and he would give places in the Bible that restoration of everything Satan had taken was promised in God's Word, the Bible.

He said, "My friend, I have good news for you today. God wants you to know that it's not over."

"Our God is a God of restoration, and he is most able and willing to restore whatever you have lost."

"How much more we who are under the new covenant of grace—a far better covenant with God based on better promises (Hebrew 8:6)—can trust God not just for 120% restoration, but much more."

"Your best days are ahead of you."

"Despite how impossible the situation looks, God is for you and will never give up on you."

"When you put your trust in Him, nothing in your life is beyond restoration."

Wow! The picture of getting back all that the enemy has stolen from us would certainly line up with progress in spite of the lack of struggle. I could not help but think of us striving and realized that with rest, all striving would cease. We could see God prospering us financially, spiritually, and physically and know that in every area of our lives would be restored, and we would know victory.

God is going to give back to us all that Satan took. He has robbed us of our marriage, finances, and relationships and lured us into sin. But the Lord is saying, "Enough!"

The above scripture is a promising scripture.

The Lord has promised to guide, satisfy, prosper, refresh, rebuild, raise up, repair, and restore his people. Our future will be a mighty one when God restores all that Satan had taken from us.

This sounds unbelievable I know, but I believe it. Our God is a God of increase and blessing. He will hear and answer our prayers as we declare what he says about things, and then, we begin believing it.

You have read about how God was restoring our marriage. Here is how God restored our finances from our divorce.

When Darren and I were going through our divorce, we had around $37,000 in attorney fees, not to mention the money I owed my family for supporting Leah and me during separation. My dad and sisters had cashed in IRAs, stocks, and whatever they needed to help me pay for my lawyer and supported Leah and me for months, as Darren's lawyer told him not to give us any money to try to starve us out. Well, I can tell you that was not going to happen. I truly believe my family would have done anything to keep me from quitting because of money. They would have sold everything they owned to get me out of that marriage with all we deserved. Boy, Satan is good.

A few weeks after Darren and I started our reconciliation, we went with Mark and Leigh Evans to a Christian conference by Joan Hunter in Tomball. She was also preaching about it being the year of restoration. She said, as we were hearing many preachers preach, that marriages, finances, relationships, and all that Satan had stolen would be restored. We were already in the process of restoring our marriage, and I remember her really emphasizing the restoration of finances that night. She kept saying *all* the money that Satan had stolen from us would be restored. She kept saying *expect* your finances to be restored. She kept saying that it was going to happen and to watch for it.

Well, I really didn't give it much thought until the next Monday when I received in the mail a letter from the IRS saying that we had overpaid our taxes from the previous year, and we would be getting a refund check of $12,000. *What?* I called Darren and Leigh as I remembered the prophecy from Joan Hunter about expecting a restoration of any finances that Satan had stolen just that previous weekend. Well, you can imagine how I was feeling, but even though I was elated, I thought, *I will believe it when I see it.* Sure enough, a couple of months later, we were pulling out of our driveway on a Sunday morning headed to church and Leah said, "Stop, let me get the mail." Well, I can honestly tell you this was the first and last time Leah has stopped us on the way out to check the mailbox, not ironic but a God thing. I assure you the Holy Spirit prompted her to check the mail that morning. Can you guess what was in the mailbox that Sunday morning? Yes, a check from the IRS for $12,000. Then, for the next few months, we kept getting refund checks for the five previous years that we had overpaid our taxes. And *yes,* they all added up, almost to the penny, the $37,000 we had paid our attorneys for our divorce. That was truly a blessing from God, giving us back the finances that Satan had stolen from us. God always does what he promises, but we have to do our part. We had done what God wanted us to do. We reconciled and were working on our marriage.

I will be totally honest with you—working on our marriage was not easy. There was a lot of damage done and a lot to repair. It was hard work, but worth every minute of it. We went to counseling at our church with our pastor and his wife at Lifehouse Bible Church. I did many Bible studies. Darren did AA, and I did Alanon. It took time, commitment, and the desire to make our marriage work. It's what God wanted. Our marriage today is the best it has *ever* been because we have God in the center of it, totally dependent on him for our every need for our joy and happiness do not come from each other. It comes from our love for our Lord and our commitment to *him.*

Chapter 28

A Life of Overflowing Blessings

The thief comes only to steal and kill and destroy; I came
that they may have life, and have it abundantly.

—John 10:10

How much does God want to bless us? In the past, I thought that God only wanted to bless us in small ways. We live as if there are limits to what is possible.

But the Bible gives us a completely different perspective. Jesus said that he came that we might have life and have it "abundantly." In his translation, I think that this literally means having life "till it overflows," blessings without limits!

Think about this: God wants you to have overflowing blessings! The question is, what are your expectations? What do you really believe about the gospel? Have you placed limits on what God can do for you? Are you dominated by doubt or hindered by fear?

Fortunately, you don't have to wonder what God would say about these matters. His Word gives you the specific answers! Just think about these truths and declare them in your life.

Jesus came "to destroy the works of the devil" (1 John 3:8). This means you already have power over every form of spiritual opposition. You can live in total victory!

If you ask in faith, anything will be possible for you.

If you have faith the size of a mustard seed,
you will say to this mountain, "Move from here
to there," and it will move; and nothing will be
impossible to you. (Matthew 17:20)

He has given you His power and authority.
(Luke 9:1)

In your life, don't place limits on God. Remember Jesus's Words, "Whatever you ask in My name, that will I do, so that the Father may be glorified in the Son. If you ask Me anything in My name, I will do it" (John 14:13–14). Believe in God's promises and expect His overwhelming blessings to flow into your life.

I sure see the truth in God's Word and promises in *my* life. The past three years since Darren and I reconciled, we have truly been blessed. Shortly after we reconciled our marriage, we sold our home without even putting it on the market. We made enough money to purchase land and build another home without borrowing any money. This was huge for us, as neither of us have a retirement. We are now able to put what we were paying in a mortgage in retirement.

After we sold our home and wanted to start building, we were living in our camper and decided to take a trip—a trip that lasted twenty-eight days. We were so blessed to have an awesome manager running our business that allowed us to leave for that amount of time and not worry about how our business would run without us there. This trip was definitely a God thing. We left with only the destination of Ohio, where our middle son Dustin was working to visit him. We saw so much in that twenty-eight days. It was the best trip. It was a great time of working on our marriage and getting to know each other again—a time that I can honestly say that I fell in love again. When I stepped out in faith, being obedient to God's command, I have to tell you, my heart wasn't in it at the time. I was just doing what I heard God telling me to do. But taking that trip changed all that for me.

In God's Word, he says, "But seek ye first the kingdom of God, and his righteousness; and all these things shall be added unto you" (Mathew 6:33).

We found God's Word to be so true, and by obeying his command, we received his overflowing blessings upon our lives.

Chapter 29

In Christ We Are Broken but Whole, Scarred but Beautiful

*Yet God has made everything beautiful for its own time. He has
planted eternity in the human heart, but even so, people cannot
see the whole scope of God's work from beginning to end.*
—Ecclesiastes 3:11

WHILE WE WERE ON OUR twenty-eight-day vacation, we traveled most
of the East Coast, exploring the many beautiful beaches along the
way. It was our fourth vacation day, and we were at one of the more
private, secluded beaches near Virginia Beach. Leah, our youngest
daughter, and I ventured down the beach, eager to find at least one
intact shell for our vacation collection. We had been filling her purple
bucket with shells every day; however, they were mostly broken. As
I looked inside with little interest, I realized that these were remains
of what once were large, beautiful sand dollars, massive conchs, and
shells of all kinds.

That was just not going to work. I was determined to find one
intact large shell to bring home.

Our adventure remained unproductive as the hour went by, and
each scoop of wet sand revealed another broken shell. After reaching
down once again to sift the sand, I spotted my daughter, skipping in
my direction, holding what seemed to be the inside of a horse conch.
Her eyes, beaming with excitement, "Oh, mom, look! It is so beau-

tiful!" I picked it up and was ready to shrug, in frustration, when I heard God whisper, "Look again. It is broken and beautiful. Much like you are."

Now that I was doing Bible studies and reading the Bible every day, there are moments in life when time stands still, and my perspective turns 180 degrees to consider life from a new angle. This was one of those moments. I knelt down beside my daughter, seeing the twisted piece in her hand in a new way, broken and simply beautiful.

A flashback of life danced in my mind as I contemplated the large shell piece—shattering moments of my past and painful situations that caused me to break time and again, sin that shattered my soul until my Redeemer made me whole, broken pieces. That was me.

No, wait a minute. That *is* me.

In a moment, I realized that everything that I've ever done and ever gone through make me who I am.

"Oh, if I could ever go back!" How many times have we wasted time wishing we could go back and fix life?

On that beautiful day at the beach, holding a broken shell, I fully grasped the fact that had I never been broken, I would not have known my Savior and experienced his redeeming, restoring love. For the first time since I've known grace, I truly embraced my brokenness as beautiful. It has made me the person God created me to be.

God loves broken shells.

Because I've been broken, I have seen the ugliness of sin for what it is and invited him to cleanse me and give me a new heart. He cleanses broken shells.

Because I've been broken, I can look at my brothers and sisters with compassion when they fail. And instead of judging them with unmerciful and self-righteous pride, I extend them sympathy, forgiveness, and love. He uses broken shells.

Because I've been broken, when my neighbor is hurting, I remember the pain and remember to give and pray for them. He softens broken shells.

Because I've been broken, and although the scars shall forever be a reminder of his deliverance and undeserving grace, my heart found peace and joy in him. God restores broken shells.

Broken and beautiful, just as God has chosen to use me to proclaim his mercies and be useful in his kingdom, I have chosen to bring a bag filled with beautiful broken shells home from the beach. They will be put in a vase and placed somewhere for me to see daily—beautiful memories of lazy days at the beach with the family I love and a fresh reminder of who I am in Christ, broken, but whole, scarred, but beautiful.

> Therefore if anyone is in Christ, he is a new creature; the old things passed away; behold, new things have come. (2 Corinthians 5:17)

I have learned to surrender my brokenness to him. Because if I am his child, my hurt has a distinct purpose. Whether it is to cleanse, strengthen, or prepare me, even though I cannot see his purpose, I trust him. I can look back now and understand that in the process of breaking me, he was remaking me. And when he's done remaking that very part that was once broken, he will use me in a mighty way.

> Consider it all joy, my brethren, when you encounter various trials, knowing that the testing of your faith produces endurance. And let endurance have its perfect result, so that you may be perfect and complete, lacking in nothing. (James 1:2–4)

Chapter 30

From Grief to Grace

He heals the brokenhearted and binds up their wounds.
—Psalm 147:3

For our struggle is not against flesh and blood, but against the rulers, against the powers, against the world forces of this darkness, against the spiritual forces of wickedness in the heavenly places.
—Ephesians 6:12

BY THIS TIME, MY MARRIAGE has been fully restored. There was restoration with family members and some friends. Our finances had been restored from our divorce, and I had learned a lot. I learned a lot about addiction, God, and the Bible. I had done two years of Bible studies where I learned so much and, most importantly, that there is an invisible war with a real enemy—Satan—how to prepare for battle, and the key to spiritual victory. I was starting to put the pieces together of why our lives went so crazy several years ago.

On August 17 of this year, as soon as I walked out the door, I felt a sadness come over me, and it hung around most of the morning. Then when I opened Timehop on Facebook, there it was, the anniversary of my mother's death. I realized this sadness was grief. For the first time since her passing, I didn't let it consume me the rest of the day. I gave that sadness and grief I was feeling to God in prayer. My day got so much better after I did that.

Grief, the death of a loved one hits each one of us at some point in our lives. A special relationship gone away, leaving empty and broken hearts. Dreams with a hope and future gone in an instant. I know. I've lived it too.

At thirty-six years old, I lost my first husband to a heart attack. One month later, my grandmother passed, and two months later, my mother was diagnosed with cancer and died a few short years later.

Oh, God.

No, God! I remember shouting out at the top of my lungs.

Hopes, dreams, future—all vanished.

I would go to my children's school events, sporting events, or even the mall and see my friends with their children, their children's fathers, and grandmothers cheering them on, playing such a special part in the lives of their children and grandchildren, which my children and I were missing out on. Seeing fathers and grandmothers being able to share and be a part of my friend's children's lives caused such weeping, groaning bitterness, and anger. My heart often wondered, *Will I remain bitter and angry or will I ever get better?*

I will never forget a statement made by the facilitator of the second grief support group I attended. He started off by saying, "I want you to feel free to express whatever you feel. If you're angry, tell us. And if you're angry at God, tell us and him. He already knows anyway."

I suppose that I had thought there was this secret compartment in my brain where my thoughts were shielded from God's sight. I immediately thought to God and to myself, *Yeah, I am angry with you, God, and I don't trust you.* I quickly added, *Now, I don't want to be, but I am.*

Years later, I was brought to my knees with a second confession of anger toward my heavenly Father. I was not only upset with God for taking Dennis, the father of my children, and my mother out of my life, but also I was angered at him for leaving me here to live and grieve, to pick up the pieces, and to raise my children without them, their support, and guidance. In my mind, I seriously thought it would have been much better for God to have taken my entire family to heaven to be together with them than to leave me here to live this life without them.

I'm telling you about my anger toward God for one reason. I told God I was angry at him not just once but twice. But I never understood that I could leave that anger at the foot of the cross with him. I kept that anger. This is a key point in my story. I kept that anger instead of giving it to God and letting him console me as only a father can do. As scripture says, he will wipe away every tear from their eyes, there will be no more mourning, or crying, or pain.

Fellow mourners, I tell you, speak to God from an honest and sincere heart. Let him know how you feel and let him help you heal. But don't hold on to that anger. If only I would have left that anger at the foot of the cross and not let the anger consume me.

Scripture says, "Do not let the sun go down while you are still angry, and do not give the devil a foothold" (Ephesians 4:26–27).

Hmm.

A foothold in our lives is an open door of opportunity Satan uses to gain access. I'm pretty sure I opened the door by holding on to that anger.

The scripture cautions us to guard the door of our hearts because Satan is always looking for a way in.

> Stay alert! Watch out for your great enemy,
> the devil. He prowls around like a roaring lion,
> looking for someone to devour. (1 Peter 5:8)

Well, with my angry, bitter heart, I was an easy prey for Satan; and let me tell you, he came in and devoured us all. We had the doors and windows wide open, with a welcome sign, saying, "Come on in."

At that time in my life, I was so angry at God that I quit going to church, I quit going to Bible studies, and I quit praying. I certainly didn't know about the armor of God and how to fight Satan, so Satan was winning. I didn't stand a chance because I had no idea the real enemy was Satan, working in all our lives.

This went on for several years; my family was falling apart. I hit my rock-bottom when Darren and I were going through our divorce, and my health was seriously declining. I didn't think I was going to make it. I had nowhere else to look but up. I cried out to God, on my knees, begging him to help me. And for the first time in years, I started hearing from the Holy Spirit again, and God started answering prayers. I felt like there was most definitely a spiritual war going on those last few months of our separation—a spiritual war, good against evil. God was working on us trying to show us the way, but Satan was using us as puppets on a string, controlling all the *craziness*.

> For our struggle is not against flesh and blood, but against the rulers, against the powers, against the world forces of this darkness, against the spiritual forces of wickedness in the heavenly places. (Ephesians 6:12).

Many times, we don't realize Satan has gotten a foothold until anger stares us in the eyes and says, "Here I am, now what are you going to do about it?" We can choose to ignore it, be afraid of it, or engage in spiritual battle and fight with the armor God provides for us in his Word.

A good starting point is to take a look at our thoughts and emotions. Is there anger we harbor? A situation we replay over and over in our mind, causing untold anger? A wound that is still sore, years later?

These are indicators of unresolved anger—anger that has been carried from one day to the next to the next, maybe even for a lifetime. The enemy uses these open doors to come between us and God, tear apart relationships, and hurt our Christian witness (John 13:35).

To avoid these destructive conditions, the scripture tells us to quickly get rid of anger so the enemy has no foothold. I don't know about you, but I don't want to live with the enemy in my life ever again.

Take your anger to the cross and leave it there.

The ones who lay their burdens down at the foot of the cross and give it to the Lord ease forward with hope and trust, and with the hand of Jesus holding them all the way. The Lord hears the cries of his children. He wants to help them. He wants to hear them call out to him and comfort them. He waits and watches and winces in pain as his children ignore him.

The fortunate ones who have had their ears and eyes opened are at a distinct advantage from others who have their ears and eyes closed. Their trials are a lot harder to endure, their hope distinguished, and their future bleak.

The ones filled with great faith lay "their burdens down" and know and trust that the Lord will sustain them and will provide for all their needs. So, when we cast our burdens, we are surrendering and give full rein to the *Lord*, knowing he will provide our every need and never let us be moved.

Are you ready to lay your heavy cares at the foot of the cross and leave that burden there so you can step into God's plans for you? Jesus promised, "For My yoke is easy and My burden is light" (Matthew 11:30).

Chapter 31

I Am Definitely a Sheep That Needs the Leading of a Good Shepherd, God!

He tends His flock like a shepherd: He gathers the
lambs in His arms and carries them close to His
heart; He gently leads those that have young.
—Isaiah 40:11

THE TYPE OF SHEPHERDING REFERRED to in the Bible is not the farming of fenced pasturelands, but a type of nomadic grazing. The shepherd must carefully plan the path and lead the way so that the sheep have neither too little nor too much grazing and are able to get to the water hole on time. Pastures are often lost to extreme heat, which means the shepherd has to scour the countryside in search of green grass. Several flocks of sheep are gathered together at night in a sheltered place so that shepherds can share the watches of the night, protecting the sheep from wild animals and thieves. Good shepherds are always willing to risk their lives to save their flocks from any harm, any enemy, and even from themselves.

Sheep are dumb, can never be left alone, and often stray, requiring the shepherd to find and rescue them. A shepherd never pushes his sheep but rather leads his sheep, going before them, making sure they are not walking into danger. The natural instinct of sheep is to be afraid. When faced with a dangerous situation, sheep panic and run—often into dangerous places. Without a shepherd to care for the sheep, they will not last long.

Personally, I definitely fit the profile of a sheep. I can't count the number of times I have stubbornly stuck to *my* plan, foolishly thinking it was better than God's plan, only to end up in some pit somewhere, calling for help. Psalm 40:1–3 has become my life maxim, with one exception. I rarely wait patiently! Remember that I am a sheep!

> I waited patiently for the *Lord*; He turned to me and heard my cry. He lifted me out of the slimy pit, out of the mud and mire; He set my feet on a rock and gave me a firm place to stand. He put a new song in my mouth, a hymn of praise to our God. Many will see and fear and put their trust in the *Lord*. (Psalm 40:1–3, NIV)

I sometimes allow fear to drive me to a place where I am trapped by doubts and darkness until he rescues me. I try to satisfy my hunger by eating the wrong things found in the wrong places at the wrong times. The result is always the same—my soul remains ravenous for what is good while stuffing my heart and mind with what is bad.

Like every sheep, I don't like to be pushed. Good shepherds do not push, no matter how great the temptation. A good shepherd stands in front of his sheep, gently calling their names, leading them to a place where he has already been, positioning himself between danger and his sheep.

When I am tired and ready to give up, I tend to withdraw from the other sheep and even from my Shepherd. Many of us have somehow bought into the lie that we can make it on our own or that the rules, the commandments of God, do not necessarily apply to us, just those other sheep. The longer I serve God, the more I realize just how much we need each other and how much we need him. When will I learn that I cannot do life on my own, as a sheep or as a shepherd?

I am so glad Jesus was willing to lay down his life for every single sheep—the cute, fluffy ones, and the dirty, broken lambs like me. Maybe it is time for us all to stop, listen for his voice, seek his plan, and remember that we are indeed needy sheep, called to love and lead other needy sheep to the Good Shepherd, Jesus Christ.

Chapter 32

Submit Yourself to God: Satan Will Flee

Submit yourselves therefore to God. Resist the
devil, and he will flee from you.

—James 4:7

I HAVE TO SAY, THIS has become one of my favorite Bible verses, and I find myself sharing it with others quite often. In it, you see the power God gives us through him over the devil. If we submit ourselves to him, then the devil, our adversary, has no power over us, but instead must flee. You know so many times people allow the devil to seduce them through temptation, which is a slippery slope. Now, granted none of us will ever be perfect, but to avoid sin, we must avoid temptation. The Word clearly states in the Lord's Prayer that we are to pray to not be led into temptation (Matthew 6:13). Therefore, by praying to avoid temptation, we should be actively living lives that don't compromise our lives as Christians. We need to examine ourselves by the Word; and yes, it may hurt; but believe me, it is for our good. Remember God chastises those who are his and those he loves. It is done for our good and to strengthen us for what is ahead.

What I also find awesome is how no temptation will ever come upon us that is too strong for us and that God will always provide a way out (1 Corinthians 10:13). The only way man ever gets caught by temptation is by his own lust and not because God didn't help him (James 1:14). Friends, be encouraged to know that the devil has no power over you unless you give it to him. Jesus Christ paid the ultimate price on Calvary, and through him, you can do all things (Philippians 4:13), even resist that old serpent, the devil.

It's really so easy. Ask God into your heart and admit you are in need of him. Be real with him and cast all your worries, doubts, and fears at his feet, the feet of mercy for he cares for you (11 Peter 5:7). Repent of your old ways and find your identity in Jesus Christ (2 Corinthians 5:17). Don't let your past or not being perfect get in the way (Psalm 103:12; Romans 3:23). Instead, cast yourself upon his mercy (Luke 18:13). Remember that He is waiting on you with arms wide open (John 3:16). In those arms, you will find love (John 15:13), mercy (Romans 5:6–8), forgiveness (1 John 1:9), and a grace that is sufficient (2 Corinthians 12:9). Will you choose him? Will you let him set you free from the bondage of Satan?

I truly saw this happen, before I read the verse James 4:7. I saw this with my husband and his addiction to alcohol and meth. He gave his life to the Lord almost four years ago, and in doing so was able to resist the temptation of his addiction of drugs and alcohol (Satan); and through the power of God, God won; therefore, Satan had to flee.

It was such an "Aha! Boom Satan" for me when I was doing a Bible study, and this verse was used. I saw so clearly this verse come to life, through my husband, giving his life to Christ, and his temptation for drugs leave.

God is so good, and his Word is so true, for yesterday, today, and tomorrow!

Chapter 33

I'm No Longer a Slave to Fear, I Am a Child of God

But one thing I do: Forgetting what is behind and straining toward what is ahead, I press on toward the goal to win the prize for which God has called me heavenward in Christ Jesus.
—Philippians 3:13–14

Forget the former things; do not dwell on the past. See, I am doing a new thing! Now it springs up; do you not perceive it? I am making a way in the wilderness and streams in the wasteland.
—Isaiah 43:18–19

THE MEMORY CAN BE TRICKY. I can't remember what I walked into a room for. I can't remember where I put my glasses. I have to write down everything I want to remember. That way, instead of spending a lot of time trying to remember what it is I wrote down, I spend the time looking for the paper I wrote it down on.

Even though I have typical problems with my memory, my past shows up unexpectedly in my dreams. While I'm sleeping, I will experience, in living color, some drama from the past that evokes a deep emotional response. The spirit of fear comes over me, and I remember those horrific encounters from those days.

But the anxieties those dreams stir up in me seem so real that I wake up breathing hard and to a full-blown panic attack. It feels like there is somewhere in my subconscious mind a recorder that won't stop replaying some things I would like to forget. It not only goes back to real events in my life but also creates scenes that reawaken old fear. It has the power to hit "replay" and not only interrupt my sleep but also disturb my days.

My conclusion is that even though I have memory problems when I'm awake, my past anxieties are still buried somewhere in my subconscious. What do I do when those old feelings bubble to the surface of my mind? Paul's advice to the Philippian believers is the answer,

> But one thing I do: Forgetting what is behind and straining toward what is ahead, I press on toward the goal to win the prize for which God has called me heavenward in Christ Jesus. (Philippians 3:13–14)

Interestingly, Paul wrote, "This one thing I do" and then mentioned two things. It must mean that those two actions are so connected that they can't be done alone. We can't strain toward something without forgetting what is behind. Wow, what a thought!

We can't focus our minds on Jesus and what he can do for us while we're focusing our minds on our past and what's been done—either good or bad. Paul wanted all of us to know that we have to lay aside our past hurts and encounters to possess our futures. Listen to the terms he used to describe the future we're to pursue. We strain toward, the goal, to win the prize for which God has called, heavenward in Christ Jesus. Whatever those things behind were, we're to focus on God and the goal he has for us in Christ Jesus. We can't look both ways at once. That's why turning from the things behind is something we are to do. If I come to the cross and lay these horrific memories down there, I don't have to lug old, negative memories with me into tomorrow.

Thankfully, one of the things we can put behind us is our emotional pain. We have each been hurt. But we can move on from that pain and whatever caused it to a bright future. We don't want to look back because, as every runner knows, when we look back, we slow down.

Forgetting doesn't mean, of course, that we wipe out our memories. I think we must sometimes remember so we can learn from our mistakes. For me, I need to remember so next time, I will let God handle my battles, instead of trying to handle and control them myself. God is so much better at going to battle for me. When I try to handle or control my problems or the problems of others, I create a big ol' mess, which has put me into some pretty dangerous situations. These situations then created these horrid memories and the spirit of fear.

This means we make a conscious decision not to let the past absorb our attention and hinder our progress. If we can move from this day to the next by choosing to be free from our past, we will be positioned to focus on the future and what God has in mind for us.

Instead of being consumed with past horrible memories, we can depend on Jesus,

> But one thing I do: Forgetting what is behind and straining toward what is ahead, I press on toward the goal to win the prize for which God has called me heavenward in Christ Jesus. (Philippians 3:13–14)

What Jesus is and what he's done will free us from our bondage of horrible memories and fears.

I recently heard this, and it speaks volumes, "Worry and fear does not empty tomorrow of its sorrow. It empties today of its strength." There's a better way. We can forget the things behind and spend our energies straining toward what is ahead.

We can't control things that happened in the past, but we can focus on the miracles around us today.

We can't control the actions that once shaped our hearts, but we can replace them with truth from the scripture.

I'm reminded of this song that has helped me release those fears that have been weighing me down and keeping me from moving forward.

> You unravel me, with a melody
> You surround me with a song
> Of deliverance, from my enemies
> Till all my fears are gone
> I'm no longer a slave to fear
> I am a child of God
> I'm no longer a slave to fear
> I am a child of God

There is so much hope! Just as the Prophet Isaiah describes new roads in the desert and rivers in the wilderness, as we give up what we can't control, to embrace what we can change, new ways of thinking, relating and living are carved into our very being.

And the beautiful thing about choosing to let go of that fear, it changes us. It positions us for the future God has for us. It allows us to press on toward the goal to win the prize for which God has called me "heavenward in Christ Jesus."

Chapter 34

Today Surrender to God
Delayed Obedience Is Disobedience

I will hasten and not delay your commands.
—Psalm 119:60

Delayed obedience is disobedience and leaves
us exposed to the enemy's advances.

I LEARNED A LOT FROM my grandchildren. Kason, our just three-year-old grandson, came up with what I thought was a genius plan for disobedience.

Yesterday, I told Kason that it was time to put away his toys and get ready. His mom was coming back from the dentist and was going to take him to school. He stopped what he was doing, and I could tell he was seriously thinking about what I had asked him to do. Then, his eyes sparkled, and he let out a huge sigh. It was obvious he had made a decision. Kason then smiled sweetly and said, "No, tank you, MawMaw. Maybe tomorrow!"

Maybe tomorrow.

I often do the same thing when God asks me to do something. I want to obey him. But right now, it is inconvenient, and I just don't want to do it. Maybe tomorrow I will.

I wonder.

Did Jesus question God or wonder why he had agreed to such a ridiculous plan? Seriously, he gave up heaven for earth, a throne for a manger, to live among frail humanity bent on self-destruction, to suffer and die for people who hated, tortured and betrayed him and thought he was nothing more than a fraud?

Did Jesus find it hard to obey God?

If I am brutally honest, I tend to think the obedience of Jesus came a lot easier to him than it does to me. After all, he was fully God and fully man—something my skeptical mind and doubting heart simply can't comprehend.

That is when I play the God card. Really, how hard could it have been for Jesus to obey God? How could he give in to temptation? He was God.

But he was also man.

> During the days of Jesus' life on earth, He offered up prayers and petitions with fervent cries and tears to the one who could save Him from death, and He was heard because of His reverent submission. Son though He was, He learned obedience from what He suffered. (Hebrews 5:7–8)

God did not give Jesus the power to obey simply because he was his Son. Jesus learned obedience the same way we must learn obedience—through desperate cries for strength to make the right choices and through tears of anguish and repentance when we make the wrong choices.

Jesus found the strength to obey God through a holy and radical submission to God. He learned obedience through pain and suffering. The word *learned* indicates a continual choice and the ongoing process of falling down, learning the lesson each failure holds, and getting back up again—determined to make the right choice. And we must do the same, knowing and willingly accepting the fact that surrender is costly, painful, life-changing, and worth it all.

I have struggled with being obedient to God's command when it doesn't feel comfortable for me. I had forgiven the people that I felt had betrayed me while Darren and I were going through our divorce. I had forgiven the friend that pulled a gun on me threatening to kill me. I had forgiven Darren's family member who was dealing drugs, who also threatened to have me killed if I didn't keep my mouth shut. Forgiving and forgetting were two different things. I had a fear of letting these people back into my life. I had some really big trust issues.

I began hearing God tell me it was time to do the forgetting and trying to mend these relationships, but I really didn't feel it. I would ask myself *why*. But I have found that I don't need to know *why*. I just need to obey and do as I hear the Lord commands.

Once I moved on what I heard God command about restoring these friendships, I felt so much peace in my life. There is such a freedom when you forget what's been done to you and move on. In doing this, you unlock the door to your full, unbridled, joy that enables you to go on and simply enjoy your life without carrying a ball and chain around.

As my youngest daughter always reminds me, you can't move forward when you're looking in the rearview mirror.

Finding out who you are is the ultimate freedom. If you define yourself by your past, you will be living as a fraction of what is possible for you, say, you think of yourself as wronged, betrayed, or victimized.

Defining yourself by what happened doesn't help you now. It's like wearing clothes that never fit. It's time to take them off.

It's easy to believe in a mistaken identity. It feels so true to think we are a result of what happened or the sum total of our thoughts and feelings. But the truest thing about you is that you are aware. Life presents a passing array of experiences—thoughts, emotions, events, and people. These all arise in you but are not you.

I have learned through the years to live as the awareness that I am fully alive, here, not in conflict with anything. Knowing who I am, a child of God, the pain of the past is barely a ripple on the surface of the immeasurable vastness of me.

God's truth is for today—not tomorrow.

Chapter 35

Closed for Renovations

I will restore David's fallen shelter—I will repair
its broken walls and restore its ruins.

—Amos 9:11

And this is the plan: At the right time he will bring everything together
under the authority of Christ—everything in heaven and on earth.

—Ephesians 1:10

God, your God, will restore everything you lost; he'll have compassion on
you; he'll come back and pick up the pieces from all the places where you
were scattered. No matter how far away you end up, God, your God,
will get you out of there and bring you back to the land your ancestors
once possessed. It will be yours again. He will give you a good life and
make you more numerous than your ancestors. God, your God, will
cut away the thick calluses on your heart and your children's hearts,
freeing you to love God, your God, with your whole heart and soul and
live, really live. And you will make a new start, listening obediently to
God, keeping all his commandments that I'm commanding you today.
God, your God, will outdo himself in making things go well for you:
you'll have babies, get calves, grow crops, and enjoy an all-around good
life. Yes, God will start enjoying you again, making things go well
for you just as he enjoyed doing it for your ancestors. But only if you
listen obediently to God, your God, and keep the commandments and

*regulations written in this Book of Revelation. Nothing halfhearted
here; you must return to God, your God, totally, heart and soul,
holding nothing back. This commandment that I'm commanding
you today isn't too much for you, it's not out of your reach. It's not on
a high mountain - you don't have to get mountaineers to climb the
peak and bring it down to your level and explain it before you can
live it. And it's not across the ocean - you don't have to send sailors out
to get it, bring it back, and then explain it before you can live it.*
—Deuteronomy 30:3–13

Type the word *RESTORE* into an Internet search engine, and links
to many different websites will appear. You can find information on
how to restore a classic car, an old piece of furniture, or an antique
piano. Every restoration project involves more than making something look new on the outside, but new on the inside as well. A
restored ship has to be seaworthy, to withstand the crashing waves
from the storms, and a restored house must become a home.

Have you ever seen a completely restored classic car cruise down
the street? It catches your eye. You think, *That's awesome! That is
beautiful! That is incredible!* That is because you love to see something restored to its original condition. I have seen many old classics
car interiors get restored after the exteriors were restored, at Cy-Fair
Upholstery. It's an amazing process to watch this project come
together.

My late husband, Dennis, loved restoring old things. His pas-
sion was restoring old Coke machines. He would take them completely apart, sand, bond the holes in the metal, and sand again and
then repeat till the metal was perfectly smooth and unflawed. Then,
he would paint the machine to match its original color. Then he
would rewire it so it would work again. This process took months,
sometimes years. But when he was done, it worked perfectly and
in some cases better than the original. I will never forget putting a
nickel in one of these newly restored Coke machines, and when the
Coke came out and you popped the top off the bottle, the top half
would freeze like ice. That particular machine, in my opinion, was
restored to better than "like new" condition. Just what Jesus wants to

do with us, restore the broken pieces in our lives and sometimes to "better" than what we were before.

Wow, I have been married to two men in the restoration business. And my heavenly Father is the master of restoring *all* things.

I like to think of myself like that old classic car or Coke machine, being restored to better than original condition by my heavenly Father. The past three years, God has been restoring and healing me from all my past hurts and anger. He has sanded and bonded the holes in my life from hurt and anger by applying his Word through the many Bible studies I have been doing. His Word acted as a salve to my wounds and healed me. I have wanted to be the person I was at thirty-six years old, prewidow—the time in my life that I felt whole. I kept comparing my life from being thirty-six years old and being fifty, trying to figure out what was missing. *How could I find that peace and happiness I once had?* It was letting go of past hurts and anger that got me to the place I could actually hear God again. Reminds me of the lyrics from *Frozen*,

Let it go
Let it go
Can't hold it back anymore
Let it go
Let it go

God's Word has something for us *all*. A road map to get your through *all* your hard times. He is waiting for us all to grab his hand, to let him pull us out of that deep dark valley of confusion and being lost.

Once all things are restored in our lives, it brings such peace— peace brought about by God himself. It happens when the Creator himself takes possession of what is rightfully his and hangs a sign over the weary that says, "Under new management."

Christ will bring lasting peace. When God restores his people, they fulfill God's original purpose for them. But there's something unique about God's restoration project. Most often, when something is restored, it is returned to its original condition. When God restores his people, he doesn't just bring them back—he brings them back better, and he also carries them forward.

Heavenly Father, I thank you that you care for all of your children. I thank you for all you have restored in my life. You restored my marriage, my family, and my finances. And now, I see you restoring friendships. You promise these things, and I have seen firsthand your Word to be true.

Chapter 36

I Finished Well,
It Is Well with My Soul

*And after you have suffered a little while, the God of all
grace, who has called you to his eternal glory in Christ, will
himself restore, confirm, strengthen, and establish you.*
—1 Peter 5:10

*God is our refuge and strength, an ever-present help in trouble.
Therefore we will not fear, though the earth give way and the
mountains fall into the heart of the sea, though its waters roar and foam
and the mountains quake with their surging. Be still, and know that I
am God; I will be exalted among the nations, I will be exalted in the
earth. The Lord Almighty is with us; the God of Jacob is our fortress.*
—Psalm 46:1–3, 10–11

IN EVERYTHING WE DO, WHETHER we choose it or not, there is a finish point—the day we graduate from school, the day the last baby leaves the nest, the time we put a completed check mark next to a goal or a to-do list, and the assignments given to us by God.

But how we finish our season is so important, and sometimes, can be life-changing.

If we quit before it's finished or run defeated to the finish line, we might miss the strength that awaits us.

Beneath the layers of fear when a season is ending, or not going according to our plans, is this thread of courage from our God. God sees our efforts and hard work in each season as he prepares us.

But how we finish might be where the blessings come, for being obedient and following God's command.

Our key verse offers each of us a little hope, a little determination, a little strength to keep going:

> And after you have suffered a little while, the God of all grace, who has called you to his eternal glory in Christ, will himself restore, confirm, strengthen, and establish you. (1 Peter 5:10)

I overcame the temptation to give up and to sign the divorce papers. I overcame the desire to give up by the strength of God. I was in a season of my life where I was so discouraged and saw no hope for us. I was ready to give up and move on. But I followed God's command to reconcile my marriage, and Christ restored, strengthened, and established us for him.

While it was tempting to quit before it was finished, I held onto the faithfulness of God, and because of that faithfulness of God and being obedient to his commands, I finished well!

Although the words "it is well with my soul" are not found in the scripture, Jesus did say, "Come to me, all you who are weary and burdened ... and you will find rest for your souls" (Matthew 11:28–29). Our compassionate heavenly Father gives us comfort, hope, and peace through his Son Jesus Christ.

Every assignment or season God calls us to offers an eternal perspective. And sometimes I have a hard time remembering this through my thoughts. But as I'm holding onto our verse, I'm reminding my soul there was restoration, confirmation, and strength that came my way because I moved my feet when God told me to move into the direction of reconciling my marriage.

It was a long season of change, deliverance, and transformation. But by the grace of God, I made it. I finished well, and it is well with my soul!

This hymn is a beautiful expression of worship—"Praise the Lord, praise the Lord, O my soul." Each verse contains wonderful expressions of faith and truth. In spite of the horrible tragedy, the comfort that comes from a strong faith in God shines brightly through the gloom. This hymn echoes not only of pain and suffering but also of the eternal hope that all believers have.

It is well with my soul.
Our scars are a sign
Of grace in our lives
And Father, how You brought us through
When deep were the wounds
And dark was the night
The promise of Your love, You proved
Now every battle still to come
Let this be our song
It is well (it is well)
With my soul (with my soul)
It is well, it is well with my soul
Weeping may come, remain for a night
But joy will paint the morning sky
You're there in the fast
You're there in the feast
Your faithfulness will always shine
Now every blessing still to come
Let this be our song
It is well (it is well)
With my soul (with my soul)
It is well, it is well with my soul
You lead us through battles (You lead us through battles)
You lead us to blessing (You lead us to blessing)
And You make us fruitful (You make us fruitful)
In the land of our suffering, God
And it is well, it is well with my soul
It is well (it is well)
With my soul (with my soul)

It is well, it is well with my soul
I trust Your ways (I trust Your ways)
I trust Your name (I trust Your name)
And it is well, it is well with my soul
It is well, it is well with my soul, my soul

Lord, thank you for providing your strength when I felt weak and wanted to completely give up. Thank you for not giving up on me and walking with me each step of the way. With you, I finished this assignment well, and it is well with my soul.

In Jesus's name, Amen.

CPSIA information can be obtained
at www.ICGtesting.com
Printed in the USA
LVHW091333061218
599057LV00011B/479/P